Colleen,

Use this as a tool
to unleash your vibrant spirit!

UNRAVELING MADNESS

A SPIRITUAL ROADMAP TO FINDING MEANING AND PURPOSE

Much Love,

DAVID LEE SADAI

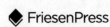 FriesenPress

One Printers Way
Altona, MB R0G 0B0
Canada

www.friesenpress.com

ISBN
978-1-03-916964-7 (Hardcover)
978-1-03-916963-0 (Paperback)
978-1-03-916965-4 (eBook)

1. BODY, MIND & SPIRIT, INSPIRATION & PERSONAL GROWTH

Distributed to the trade by The Ingram Book Company

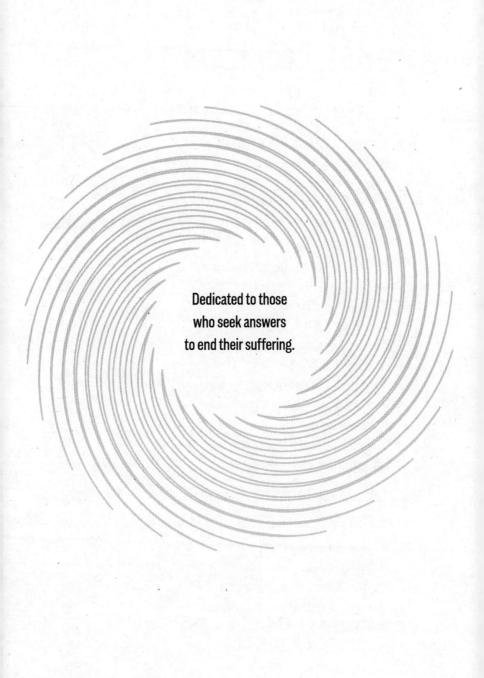

Dedicated to those
who seek answers
to end their suffering.

CONTENTS

INTRODUCTION —
THE JOURNEY WITHIN

The spiritual journey is individual, highly personal.
It can't be organized or regulated. It isn't true that everyone
should follow one path. Listen to your own truth.

—Ram Dass

WE INTUITIVELY *KNOW* that there is much more to this life than what
we have been taught and what meets the eye. We can agree that
being alive is truly the greatest gift we have ever received. However,
some of us fall into amnesia and forget about life's gift, its divinity, and sacredness when we narrowly perceive reality through
filters and dissonance that cause us to suffer in madness and live
a life untrue to ourselves. We become limited, conditioned, and
programmed to believe in illusions that sever our connections to
experiencing higher dimensions of being. Fortunately, we each
hold the power to transcend our suffering and the madness we
are intoxicated with through the spiritual journey that shifts our
awareness to seek within for answers that teach us how to unlock
ourselves to the process of our unraveling and *awakening*. We
learn about our own natural intelligence as an entity capable

I

of self-healing and evolution. In placing ourselves in elevated dimensions of consciousness, we experience more moments of resonance, presence, and stillness, that empower our emancipation and liberation to control and guide our choices and decisions toward peeling off all our layers of madness. What is beneath these layers is the purity of our spirit that is present in the moment; seeing, being, feeling, and experiencing life in connection to truth, self, love, bliss, and oneness. In this realm, you can manifest the dreams you have as they intertwine with your world and reality. The caterpillar embarks on the unknown path, the journey within, where it finds a place to enter the process of metamorphosis. In transition we go within and seek answers in aloneness, the cocoon like state. To then be reborn into the present moment evolving and transcending as the butterfly. We become free, liberated, and infinitely eternal by using our past experiences of challenge, struggle, and suffering to teach us how to become *present* and *one* with the self, reality, and universe; mind, body, and spirit.

> Spirituality is learning to turn the dissonance into resonance and shift the resonance into radiance.

Unraveling Madness is designed to be an informational spiritual roadmap to pull you out of the existential quicksand you may find yourself suffering in and help you navigate your way beyond the illusions of fear and separation and constructs like false identity, time, and money from enslaving your spirit. It offers guidance on the inner spiritual journey that reconnects you with your authentic self, your personal truth, unconditional love, and oneness with all things in the universe. The aim of this book is to help you awaken and transcend the suffering you may be experiencing through embracing a daily practice and routine that perpetually elevates your level of consciousness to the higher dimensions of being. Guiding your discovery to a process and rhythm of life that is connected and aligned with the clear, precise, and formulated plan of attack that reverse engineers the unraveling of your truest self-serving for a meaningful purpose.

You might ask: How do I get there?

In Part One, we look at the root causes for our pain and unnecessary suffering; where it originates and how it impacts, influences, and intoxicates our experience of life. By discussing these negatively influencing and low vibrational factors, we open the dialogue to begin learning how to observe life a little closer and deeper, where we can start to put a face to our layers of suffering and *recognize* the illusions, lies, and constructs of madness that exist in our individual and collective realities.

Once we know and understand the rules of the game we are in, the cast of characters involved, and the playing field, we can choose a different path where we carve our own route for escape by stepping into the *unknown;* unlearning, purifying, and aligning our mind, body, and spirit to the truth and power of our self. In Part Two, we embark on a spiritual journey and process whereby we accumulate *new* knowledge and shift our focus within and show ourselves how to elevate our consciousness, elevate our energetic vibration, and grow our spiritual practice by being present in the fourth dimension of being. In this dimension we start healing and dissolving the traumas and wounds of our past story, identity, and references by expanding our perspective that teaches us connections to truths so deep that we experience profound epiphanies and personal realizations.

Then, in Part Three, we begin to apply the new knowledge gathered from the fourth dimensional spiritual journey, to transcend our once limited and narrow perspective to the infinite, eternal, and blissful super consciousness. We learn what we must *let go* of to experience the purity of the fifth dimension of being and operate our lives in awareness of self-connection and oneness. We learn to become the alchemist who transmutes our deepest sufferings into our highest vibrational energy. In the fifth dimension, we tap into a deep connection with the powerful strength of our spirit. We unravel all the psychological and physiological cycles of suffering and begin to see that suffering is only necessary in our path to show us that it is truly unnecessary. We begin to live with wisdom, knowledge, and in alignment with our true self. A life of no regret, no guilt, no shame, and no master. You begin to experience a completely different state of being that you always knew was possible but struggled to understand. In spirituality we create a portal for ourselves to experience the truth by finding the answers we seek **within**.

> Religion is for people who are afraid of going to hell.
> Spirituality is for those who've
> already been there. —Vine Deloria Jr.

This is not a simple path. There are many levels to elevate toward and many layers of madness to unravel, transcend, and let go. Sometimes it's the lowest points of our lives that can serve as the catalyst for the change that catapults us into our evolution. Robert Tew said "Everything we go through, grows you" because he understood the only direction after hitting rock bottom is up. And from that up there's the possibility to reach levels you may never have had before. This is the magic of the universe putting you through something to get your attention. So you can *wake up*. Maybe it's a major life event, a near death experience, or perhaps you've just suffered to such a degree that you have decided you are ready for a change. Chances are if you have been attracted to this book, you are ready to do things differently. Let's use this opportunity together to go over the ways to recalibrate our self and life.

I had one very life-altering moment where I realized I was pushed to the very edge of my sanity from all the suffering I was experiencing. I had gotten to a point where I was contemplating taking my own life. These thoughts about taking away this hell I was experiencing by ending my own life were coming to my focus increasingly. I was deep enough in my own misery that I had brought myself to make a choice to either end the suffering by ending my life or take a journey to do everything necessary to climb my way out of the hole I dug myself into. I woke up one day and decided that I had had enough of experiencing my life in such a torturous, monotonous, and aimless way. I decided to handle being knocked down by life differently when I intentionally and deliberately chose to face my greatest fears and impediments by following the guidance of my heart down the path of the unfamiliar and unknown. It started with such a simple thought that it blossomed into a wild adventure.

I remember laying on my cot while on a leadership course with the army. I was a twelve-hour drive from home, in a different province, missing my family, and in an environment filled with alpha males and high stress. Many factors in my life were pulling me deeper and deeper into experiencing depression, anxiety, apathy, and anger. The thought popped into my mind while I was staring up at the ceiling: "Why am I miserable?" I sat with this question for a while because it hit me so differently than ever before. My mind became insatiably curious as to what the true answer for why it was that I was carrying so much guilt, resentment, regret, sadness, nervousness, stress, anger, and self-loathing. I wondered why my mind would tell me so many self-defeating and self-sabotaging things that caused me to feel so low about who I was, what I was doing, and question why I was even alive. I had questioned the cause of my misery before, but this time my mind opened in a way that was ready to do something *different* to change this tired, pathetic, and uninspired life I was experiencing. My biggest issue moving forward was that in the past whenever I would try to fend off my inner critic and move things in my life toward the right direction, I would only find a temporary momentum for happiness that would inevitably cycle me back into *wavering* and wallowing in my circumstance. I could never achieve a significant enough breakthrough where I could get my state of being and direction for life in alignment and keep hold of it long enough to see things through. I was mentally, physically, and spiritually exhausted from carrying the weight of the past while chasing happiness in all the wrong directions.

I needed a new route of escape from this hell. I needed something different from what I had already tried or from what the various religious teachings offered. I needed my own religion. So, after asking myself "Why am I miserable?" and not wanting to end up as another sad story of someone ending their own life, I shifted into a new direction and set out on a deliberate and intentional spiritual journey that guided me to find the answers for my mental, physical, and spiritual suffering. I knew that pain was inevitable, but suffering was the choice. I chose to pick my pain to have a why, a reason for what I sacrifice for. I wanted the pain of early mornings, long meditations, challenging work, facing my fears, and guiding myself toward a meaningful purpose rather than the pain of sleeping in, hiding in comfort, suffering, aimlessness and living without meaning.

I had to do something that I had never done before, so I shifted my focus within.

The day after questioning my misery, a friend on the base asked me to take a trip with him out to Lloydminster, Saskatchewan to get away and have a break from army life. I jumped at the idea of escaping my existential crisis and was completely unaware of the monumentally powerful shift that my life was about to take. While my friend was shopping around for a new phone, I had a strange intuitive pull to go to the bookstore within the mall we were at. I was thinking about how I had just finished reading the first book I had read in years, The "Education of a Bodybuilder" (Schwarzenegger, Hall, 2016) by Arnold Schwarzenegger and I enjoyed it mostly for the life philosophy, the fact that it inspired me to think new thoughts and provided me with ideas and opportunities to grow in new ways. I decided for this next book to target my issue a little more directly by looking in the self-help section to continue the habit.

I was nervous stepping down the self-help aisle at first. Here I was a "tough infantry army guy" about to become a leader and looking around for answers to my mental, emotional, and spiritual problems. I stepped into the fear of being judged about this and felt courage for bringing myself to do it. As soon as I began looking around on the shelf for something that would catch my eye, there it was; I saw a black and yellow title jump out at me that felt like destiny as it read:

*"I used to be a miserable f*ck" (Kim, 2019)*

I took this as a universal sign. I could not believe this book was implying the past tense of experiencing misery which was the *exact* same issue I was struggling with. I remember thinking that I wanted to be able to say that I *used* to be a miserable fuck too! I gave the book a chance and from reading, it opened my eyes for the first time to the deeper layers of my problems and issues. This book officially kicked off my spiritual journey because I quickly realized it gave me information, knowledge, wisdom and better than all that personal proof that I could do something about the misery I was experiencing. My world really became wider the moment I realized that there had to be so many other books and resources out there that I could find and get my hands on, learn, and then apply to help me get past my limitations, barriers, and blockages. Upon realizing everything I dreamed of coming true was just a matter of figuring out the universal cosmic formula,

I made a promise to myself to channel my inner lion and hold myself responsible to hunt for all the answers I seek. To leave no stone unturned until I was living an inspired life, with purpose, meaning, and true self connection.

I began my journey under an avalanche of illusion. I had a zoomed in perception that would focus on depression, being paralyzed by traumatic memories of the past, and crippled by deeply conditioned thoughts of anxieties and intense fears. I was carrying around a story that held a heap of sabotaging reactions, grudges, intolerances, judgements, references, and toxic vocabulary and language.

I was suffering under these thoughts and illusions because I was never willing to dive deeper than surface level and face my own fears long enough to investigate and get answers to these questions. I realized that I was suffering because I was living as the consequence of my past circumstances.

This journey for me started when I had a conversation with myself in the mirror and realized:

I did not like the way I was feeling.

I did not like the way I was thinking.

I did not like the way I was living my life.

I had no meaning or purpose behind anything I was doing.

But I was ready to do whatever it took to change this.

At this pivotal moment, I realized the fork in the road where I could heal the wounds that were causing me to experience life in this way. I knew that the way I was thinking, feeling, and living was not sustainable nor congruent with the truth of who and what I *really* am. I knew there had to be more than life than this. Once taking steps down this journey, I began to slowly connect to the divine energy within all of us. The higher consciousness of love, bliss and oneness beyond the limitations and categories of our identity, story, sex, nationality, race, gender, or job title. I could connect to the sacred, the divine and the *unworldly*. I knew at this point why I had to live, I had to share my story.

I desired to live connected with my own truth. I realized that the problem was that I believed the identity and story of my past and the future where nothing would be beautiful. I was living my life looking in the rear view of everything that has happened causing me to be unable to be in the now and confidently make decisions and choices that would evolve and grow me toward a future myself and truth desired. I was not present with myself and life steering the wheel and pushing the buttons. I lacked freedom and control.

I did not live in my own self referenced truth because I was blinded by living according to everyone else's. I had accepted the dissonance I was born and raised into, a false perception of self and reality that lacked connection and blocked me from experiencing states of bliss and true unconditional love.

Within all of us, some part knows there is more to it than led on. I authored this book to give you access to the knowledge and information that helped me find myself, meaning, and purpose, so that you too can use it to *awaken*.

Our beliefs form our perception. Our perception influences our state of being. Our state of being creates our experience. So, what we believe is the reality we perceive and experience. When our beliefs are disconnected by dissonance and we are in amnesia of our true self, we perceive reality in blindly accepted lies and illusions and consequently, suffer through our experience of life.

> What are your true beliefs?
> What is the reality you perceive?
> Is your state of being true to yourself?

SELF-RESPONSIBILITY

You are the hero you have been waiting for.

Before we begin, it is important to understand that you must accept and claim an elevated level of responsibility and hold yourself accountable in this journey and process. It is from the foundation of our self-responsibility that we can decide and choose to commit ourselves to the *discipline* and *consistency* required to endure the necessary challenges and progressions that bring lasting and profoundly meaningful changes to our life. None of the information from this book will help you if you do not commit to being responsible for yourself. This journey and process comes with its highs and lows, victories and setbacks, fears, and unknowns, so you must be clear with yourself about the level of responsibility and commitment you have, to build your strength and endurance for the days that are not easy or when you do not want to do it.

We must not rely on our friends, family, governments, corporations, pharmaceutical companies, or politicians to fix our own problems. This journey shows us the power of aloneness where we can clear everything out of the way and hear our truth and self. It must be you who disappears to enter the cocoon that transforms you into the butterfly. It must be you that unplugs from the matrix and disconnects from the mind that is wired to suffer. It must be you that elevates your skills, abilities, perspective, and self-connection so that you can reimagine life as the highest version of yourself. You must become responsible for the challenging work, daily practice, and routine that perpetually evolves you toward a meaning and purposeful life filled with moments of magic, adventure, and *aliveness*.

It can help to create a daily affirmation, vision board, follow a mantra, or intention to claim your high-level awareness for self-responsibility so that it remains *always* with you in your presence throughout this journey.

There is an incredible affirmation exercise that I suggest you implement right away that will help shift you to become responsible on this spiritual journey. It works by harnessing the universal power of 3:6:9 where we surround our entire focus towards thinking, looking and being intentional in all the ways that first attract then manifest anything you dream or desire. For cycles of thirty-three days, create an affirmation for yourself of something that you want to bring from un-manifest to manifest. For example, you could affirm something as simple as *"I must forgive and let go"* and watch the magic of its focus change your life especially if you notice that you are holding on to grudges that deny you from enjoying your life. Or you can use *"My challenges are opportunities"* and you will notice yourself seeking higher mountains to climb if you have been struggling to handle adversity. You can also choose to use something specific like *"I must choose opportunities to be more loving in my relationships"* or *"I will complete the goal of xyz, by this day and time"*.

Once you decide upon the affirmation to guide you, write it down each day **three** times after waking up in the morning, **six** times in the afternoon before your last meal, and **nine** times before going to bed. Having consistency and discipline with this exercise will create magic; a monumental shift in the ways you think, act, walk, speak, sleep, eat, be, and live as the power of your focus is directed and bridged to have responsibility, acceptance, and more importantly the *belief* of what you affirm.

The repetition of this daily exercise serves as a reminder for your awareness to focus on the direction you choose to place your life's energy. Life can knock us out of alignment with being responsible and focused on our path, so this exercise helps keeps you centered and dialed in especially when motivation fades. Again, we are trying to end cycles of suffering so please understand it is not always going to be easy, but through this exercise we can find harmonious ways to be consistent in our growth and evolution.

You can use this to exercise to transcend the deep wounds that hold you back, as well as set new programs for your mind by applying the wisdom of the lessons you learn while you evolve through your journey. The affirmations you choose will open your spiritual eyes toward observing everything differently and everything you observe will then begin to look different; you will ascend to the higher levels of the perceptual reality you aim to be in by aligning yourself and focus to the intentions you affirm. This exercise will show you the doors of opportunity that your awareness is seeking to prove what you affirm to become reality.

Renewing this thirty-three-day exercise will have you tap into intentionally controlling and directing the power of your mental, physical, and spiritual consciousness. By winning the war on the inside and bringing the internal control to meet with the external, your intentions of self-mastery begin to yield more moments of *resonance*. In resonance we achieve the high vibrational energetic frequency of the truth within you, to be harnessed and lived outwardly; merging the purity of life and the power of self. In resonance we remove ourselves from being our own greatest impediment and deny the outside factors that attempt to steer us away from our truth.

Realize that you *and only you* must be the hero and savior that you are waiting for. This book, amongst many other teachers and sources of knowledge, can provide information and tools, but the power to change your life is your responsibility. You must be the one to carve the path by doing the *inner* work. Nobody is going to come along and solve the problems that you have in your mind, body, and spirit. Nobody will force you to make any of the progressions necessary to heal, grow, and transcend the madness you have been intoxicated with. Stop waiting around for it to be handed to you. It must be you. Make it so.

Affirm: *I am responsible for everything in my world.*

PART ONE
THE THIRD DIMENSION OF BEING

CHAPTER ONE:
RECOGNIZING MADNESS –
THE ILLUSIONS OF DISSONANCE

YOU STAND AT a crossroads. Realizing this madness and suffering within you *must* end.

But how?

By looking within, silencing the mind, observing life a little closer, and learning to steer our own wheel, we can unlearn and unravel the madness set within our mind, body, and spirit. We can re-learn what it is to be alive in this human experience. Become aware of our awareness. We pull ourselves out of this illusionary matrix of unnecessary suffering by understanding the cause of it.

The suffering caused by living in the third dimension of consciousness means you experience:

- Conditioned and inherited mental/physical/spiritual low energetic vibrations.
- Compulsive, reactionary, unconscious, complacent, comfortable, and passive life choices.
- Distraction from practicing self-love and living your true self's desired path.

- Knowledge, perception, and personality is built under a veil of illusion that is blind from true self.
- Unhealthy conflict, competition, and comparison.
- Thoughts of madness and ego form the beliefs of your internal dialogue.
- Incantations of a false sense of identity and story.
- Paralyzed by traumas, fears, over thinking, and stress.
- Low vibrational states of being; negativity, anger, frustration, depression, anxiety, and suicidal ideation.
- Prejudice towards self and others, resistance to change, self-sabotaging attachments.
- Disconnection from the heart and mind that causes you to live and love conditionally.
- Perception is limited to only the five senses.
- Filters that cloud and narrow your perception in present moment reality.

It is important to recognize and put a face to the madness that causes our suffering. We do this by seeing the sources and factors that directly create suffering in our mental, physical, and spiritual experience of life. We will explore the third dimensional reality and use this information like sonar for detecting signs and signals of madness hiding in plain sight. Once we understand and recognize the madness within our individual and collective realities, it can be disrupted and absolved from negatively impacting our state of being, health, and energy. Let us take a closer look at the madness that pulls us away from ourselves in the third dimension of being.

THE VOICE OF MADNESS

From the moment of our birth, our mind begins building its knowledge base through a mental matrix. It collects and stores information from the communication and subtle energies that our conscious and subconscious mind picks up from our environment. Based on unique factors of what we receive from our environment and the way we receive it, our mind becomes shaped, influenced, and *epigenetically* built. This program our mind develops and uses can be shaped to work against us when it filters out high dimensions of consciousness in our perception. The most important years of our brain building its operating software are our first seven years of life. If we are shown a world that lacks connection to self and truth, we too will condition this as our routine habits, patterns, and behaviors that set the default mode for our perception. We lose our present moment connection to reality and true power of divine creation because our focus is hijacked and hypnotized into believing the lies and illusions spoken to us by our environment, we are unaware that we condition ourselves to suffer under the voice of madness. When this voice speaks to us as our internal dialogue, we assume, expect, judge, react, and habituate using a narrow frame of reference to navigate us through our experience of life.

You may hear this voice tell you a story that you are better than others, or to be prejudiced toward your own self. It tells you to distract your focus, to be sedentary or take offence. It lowers your energy, momentum, and enthusiasm instead of speaking into existence a highly vibrant life in connection with your true self. This becomes the death by a thousand cuts as each small and short-term gratifying choice and decision made denies you of the mentality and energy that guide you toward who you truly are and what you desire. Do you ever ask this voice you hear inside you if it is speaking from your deepest and most connected *truth*? Is what you think *really* what *you* think? Only if you blindly choose to believe it.

We talk ourselves into believing it is best for us to play it safe, take no risks, and choose the most comfortable path. These lies we blindly believe become the limitations in our mind that evolve to become the limitations for our experience of life. We box ourselves into prisons of believing this *story* and *identity* that the voice of madness speaks. Like the metaphorical angel and the devil that whispers in our ears, our truth is the angel, and the voice of madness is the devil.

Unlearning these programmed beliefs that do not speak our truth nor serve our highest intentions is our journey to self-freedom and liberation. In stillness, we can expand our awareness to be present, see and sense deeper, from different angles, instead of unquestionably accepting all of what we are taught and see as truth. In the *daily practice of meditation*, we can clear the mind, see these unconscious decisions, and raise our awareness to connect to ourselves and participate in our life more often. We can look within and begin to discern lies from truth. If we no longer live off the automation of our programmed mind's voice, we can see the choices and make the decisions that are congruent with our true self. Making this shift is incredibly empowering. Listen for the voice of madness within you and begin to interrupt it from accepting the lies it speaks to you by challenging its narrative through expanding your perspective.

THE POWER OF WORDS — THE SPELL OF MADNESS

Words contain spells. Each word holds a series of agreements and references for the purposes of our communication and has the power to create our reality from our mind. Words hold a heavy consequence because if misused your experience of the world and reality will be the prison that limits you. Madness consumes our mind, experience, and state of being when the words and language we use are against ourselves, against our truth, against others, and most important against love. Know that specific words and language are intentionally infused into our history, culture, and reality to divide and separate us from ourselves and each other.

It is important to know that our words and language have mutually agreed upon associations, but our problems arise because we each have different perspectives, and because everything is beyond the mere limitation of a set description, we can attach different meanings to the same word. This is the gap of our misunderstandings. If we are both looking at a piece of paper from opposite sides, I see 6 and you see 9, who is right? The illusion is that one is right, and the truth is that we both are. We can use the same word and mean two different things, and this all depends on the way we are shaped and programmed to look at and interpret it. When we try to categorize something complex or fluid with a single word for convenience and comfort, we marginalize and narrow our perception, causing us to lose the ability to perceive from multiple lenses, angles, and perspectives.

As our humanity continues to advance and evolve, with it, our words and language evolve too. You must understand the power each of us has as an equal partisan of this humanity that represents humankind by the words we humans choose and use to speak, to create and impact our individual and collective realities, as well as our mental, physical, and spiritual health and wellbeing. We can speak ourselves and each other into sickness and madness if we are not wise, present, and careful with the words we choose and use.

Do you speak the language of madness to express and paint your identity, sense of the world, and reality? It is easy to fall into the toxic mainstream use of words and language that is integrated into our social circles, work settings, sports, entertainment, and news streams. Unawareness of its influence can cause a perceptual shift within our references, thoughts, and behaviors that download the energetic messages from these low vibrational words into our mind. Our mind is constantly seeking for threats and taking in subtle subconscious elements from everything going on in our environment and reality and if without conscious strength, we can be culled into blindly accepting the words that promote bigotry, selfishness, conditional love, and forms of hate and separation.

It is particularly important on this spiritual path to take an honest assessment of the words you use in your daily internal and external experience by reflecting upon the choices we make with our words. It is wise to sit with this long enough to sift through the mind thoroughly to recognize and weed out what madness exists in your words and speech. In understanding the power of our words, we learn to become the gatekeeper of our mind. As the gatekeeper, you remain aware and protective of what is allowed in and what is allowed out. You decide to speak in ways that are only in alignment with our connection to self, truth, and love. We can choose to *replace*, *rephrase*, and *reframe* the words we notice in our communication to ourselves and the world. We must choose our words wisely and handle them with the upmost care. Handle your words like you would handle a knife.

THE FALSE SELF

A man once asked Buddha, "I want happiness," to which Buddha replied, "First remove 'I,' as that's ego. Then remove 'want' as that's desire. See now, you are only left with happiness."

When we use the term "I," what we are referencing in most moments is rarely speaking from a conscious presence that is connected and aligned with the deepest element of our powerful spirit and true self. Due to this gap, most of what "I" thinks, speaks, and experiences on behalf of our sense of identity is actually the development and compartmentalization of our illusionary false self-identity. Perceiving life through the false self, we become victims of our past circumstances through self-imposed limitations, irrational fears, and feelings of uncertainty and doubt that over time narrow our perception and box in the infinite potential of present and future possibilities. We start to believe the lies of the ego telling us things like "I can't do this," or "It's not possible for me," and because it sounds like our voice, we confuse it with our truth. This causes us to falsely believe who we think we are and forces us to become indecisive about what our true self wishes to do with our time and energy. In madness, we begin to normalize living a life untrue to ourselves which creates the opportunity for us to fall in cycles of suffering. The narrative of the illusion we are brought into and forced to go along with consumes our spiritual identity by distracting and severing our connection to our present moment awareness of true self. We suffer in the madness of the false self by living behind our masks and lies, believing we are the categories society divides us into and that the roles we play are who we *really* are. We all subjected to hearing the voice of our ego; nobody is exempt from it. It tells each of us a similar story and dialogue, that we are too this, too that, in need of praise, or make prejudice judgements for situations. We all hear this voice trying to pull us into believing this as truth and if we do not have the strength or knowledge to combat it, we become comfortable living under the illusion. In this spiritual journey, we must instead put value on our ability to self-connect and self-refer. By looking within, questioning the voice of the ego, you will see for yourself that we are so much more than the categories and limitations of a fixed identity.

On the spiritual inner journey, it is wise to begin to question everything and face our deepest fears by taking a long hard look at our ego. Recognize its shortcomings and the ways that it pulls you down and away from your authentic self. See how ego makes you become who and what you are not. Begin to ask these questions to yourself with the intent of discovering an answer:

- Where am I?
  - ▷ *Do you sometimes feel lost? Are you being pulled away from the present moment?*
- When am I?
  - ▷ *Are you burnt by the past? Worried about an unpredictable future?*
- What am I?
  - ▷ *Do you "fit in"? Is what you have done in the past really "you"?*
- How am I?
  - ▷ *Do you question the source of your existence and life?*
- *Why am I?*
  - ▷ *Do you struggle with meaning and purpose?*
- Who am I?
  - ▷ Do you see oneness? Are you the limitations you perceive?
- Are you something more?

When you take your time and energy to pursue the answers patiently and intentionally to these questions, you may find that the truth is that our identity is something beyond the fixed identity of ego. The truth is our real self is something in perpetual motion, in constant expansion and evolution. It is fluid and transitory, not fixed under the categories and classifications that mainstream culture uses to categorize and divide everything. We are something so much more than the diseases that were diagnosed, the race we have been born as, or the role we play for work. And it's that point of origin we must first reference before all these societal prisons of limitation.

THE PROGRAMMED ILLUSION

You take the blue pill...the story ends, you wake up in your bed
and believe whatever you want to believe. You take the red pill...
you stay in Wonderland, and I show you how deep
the rabbit hole goes. —Morpheus

Many spiritual traditions and Indigenous cultures have warned of the mass psychological infection-mind virus, *Wetiko,* which translates in Algonquin to *cannibalistic spirit (Laha, Kirk, 2016).* Over centuries, those who have inherited and held positions of enormous influence and power understood the mass *controlling* benefits and future possibilities of infecting the hive mind of humanity to be programmed and conditioned to the energetic vibrations of this cannibalistic spirit that blinds us to self-connection and the spiritual realm. The program of the illusions that build, shape, and influence our minds is cast out to intentionally create a humanity that primarily experiences life in the dissonance of low energetic vibrations and fearful of their survival. Consequently, this distances and outright severs our connection with ourselves and the high vibrations of our spirit because we are panic ridden about our addictions to immediate gratification and fearfully focused on keeping ourselves surviving and healthy. We in turn stop thinking and focusing on life's divinity and sacredness and develop diverse levels of amnesia of our own power as we are corralled to be lost, aimless and mentally, physically, and spiritually dependent upon the rat race matrix we live in. We become too tired from working our jobs and taking care of our responsibilities that we forget to truly *live* and instead waste our time in outlets of distraction and avoidance because we are so spiritually weakened to do anything about it. The reality is that we are closer to living on a human farm than we are a free humanity. Through manipulative attacks to our psychology and biology, there is a direct aim to limit and narrow our perceptions to living in fear, ego, and illusion so that we are divided and separated from our divinity and power by perceiving our lives through a programmed 3-Dimensional veil of illusion.

This thought-form, psychological infestation, works on emotional, vibrational, and energetic wavelengths within us to condition, program, normalize and down-regulate our individual and collective conscious and subconscious belief systems, thought patterns, habits, and behaviors to be as Jiddu Krishnamurti explains, "well-adjusted to a profoundly sick society" (Krishnamurti, 1960). We have been programmed by an illusion to accept a way of being that does not empower nor serve us individually nor collectively. Rather, it disconnects us from the very magical and enlightening experience of being alive. In illusion, we forget the sacred because we are scared. We forget the divine because we are in debt. We forget who we are because we do not know how to self-connect. We cannot see truth when we are blind.

If you observe our world and reality closely enough, you can begin to detect the illusions in the narrative and intuitively feel the presence of this negative and dark energetic force. It shows itself through physical and psychological *messages* and *symbols* hidden in everything we see and hear. The illusion forms as the walls we are imprisoned by that deny us the experience of freedom, liberation, happiness, bliss, and love. These messages and symbols gain power over us when they permeate deep enough in our minds to become our beliefs. We are mesmerized under false beliefs that we need a specific body shape, a certain title, career, material possessions or amount of money in our bank account to grant ourselves permission to be our authentic and unapologetic self that experiences love and happiness. We start to believe in the lies that the medications we take, the games we play, the alcohol we consume, or the crimes we commit will make things better. These illusions box us into believing we are only capable of small feats of achievement or impact in this world because we are stuck to the traumatized identity, we see ourselves as.

The belief in these and many other illusions deny us a life lived in truth of our self because it pushes us toward forms of separation where we focus on conflict, unhealthy comparisons, and unhealthy competition with ourselves and others. The illusion tricks us under its spell to be our own obstacle in the way by following along with the self and story of who we *think* we are but never doing any internal investigation into *knowing* who we truly are. In this degeneration of our spiritual power, we are stuck in cycles of suffering anxiety, depression, frustration, anger, and lack of life direction and meaning for what we do with our time and energy. Deeper and deeper, we fall into believing the lies that were blind to seeing. This conditioned program of madness that we are domesticated and indoctrinated to sucks the spirit right from our very *being*.

This highly organized, mass psychosis *spell* of illusions manipulates our psychology by holding our point of focus to experience the reality that is presented to us. When we do not practice connecting to the spiritual realm, of using self-referral and self-consoled references for information, knowledge, or beliefs, we open ourselves to suffer by the pull of the illusions we accept as truth.

> The illusion programs our mind to the acceptance of living in cycles of suffering.
>
> We suffer because we do not know what we do not know.
>
> You must bring it to light.

MIND PARASITES & THEIR INTELLIGENCE

A parasite is an organism that lives in or on another species (its host) and benefits by deriving nutrients at the other's expense.

There are multi-dimensional parasites around us that feast on our mind, body, and spirit as its host. This requires us to look deeper at what we may overlook, believe, and accept to begin to see and *sense* them. The base commonality that these parasites share is that they all feed off some aspect of our valuable high vibrational life-force energy. Parasites cause a negative energetic impact, usually disguised as a positive one. They attach themselves to our mind and burrow deeply into our subconscious minds, our habits, behaviors, routines, and our ego's inner voice. Parasites cause our time, focus, finances, personal growth, momentum, motivation, and high vibrational energy to be sucked dry.

Let us begin to understand the intelligence of the parasite through the tactics of the tick. Ticks use their highly evolved sense of smell to detect locations for hints of carbon dioxide. They do this because they know to go where life was present, because that is where it will be again. They understand the psychology behind the path of least resistance and exploit it for their gain. They venture to the commonly used trails of wildlife and climb up the surrounding branches and tall grass to a torso height and patiently wait. If you look down at any deer trail in a forest, you will see for yourself this web-like, tunnel vortex they use to set their trap for the unsuspecting host.

Now imagine looking for these similar types of traps in our reality. Metaphorically, our focus, our mind, and our state of being, are the unsuspecting host running down safe, familiar, patterned trails that are littered with parasites. An example of the easiest one to spot is the paid sponsorship/ commercial advertisement. While the focus is tricked to be centered around the facade of the enter- taining show, movie, or sport, it is only consequential to the main attraction; the advertising that hooks you in. Also, it is observed in this era of data collection, unassumingly selling ourselves as information as *we* turn ourselves into the product. Behind the curtain, there are teams of psychologists building the visual, auditory, and kinetic stimulating content to specifically extract chemical and emotional responses from mass amounts of people. Using the same commercial, repeating it multiple times over throughout the same show, because that is how we were taught in school. Hiring recognizable celebrities to put their trustworthy and comforting stamp of approval on products and services. There is no length to which these parasites will not go to trap impressionable minds. I wish to empower you to use this knowledge and see the deeper dimensions of reality by questioning what you observe more as you travel this journey and use it to recognize and peel away the layers of madness.

Smoking way too many cigarettes, excessive screen (TV/cell phone) use, alcohol abuse, and reckless gambling were just a few of my own parasites that I noticed draining my high vibration energy resources. Like Stockholm syndrome, I believed these things were giving me something beneficial, because they were very comforting and distracting in times of high emotional stress. They seemed "normal," as everywhere I looked, others were using these as an outlet too. These pacifying parasitic habits and behaviors became destructive to my health, wellbeing, and energy levels. I was under a superficial mask of living well, but deep inside, I knew these things were taking something from me more than they were giving back. By my energy being drained by these parasites I began unconsciously living as a passenger to my own life. Whenever a problem came up, I was conditioned to just go for a smoke, watch a show, drink some beer, laugh, avoid the problem at all costs and wake up the next day with nothing solved and my resources of money, time, and energy completely wasted. For what? How was this ever going to lead me toward a life lived as my truest self? It's so remarkable how parasites can cause ten, twenty, or even fifty years to go by in the blink of an eye.

It is important to observe all factors in your life that could be parasites to you, things that appear as "good," but in reality, are *taking* your energy from you while giving little to nothing in return. All energy in this universe works in a harmonious exchange of give and receive. If your focus, thoughts, actions, habits, and behaviors are centrally consumed by *parasites* that only take from your daily energy and do not nurture or replenish it, you will eventually run low on energy and will and suffer unnecessarily as the consequence. It is wise to find ways to fill your own cup and not just empty it. It is not wise to live this life allowing what you consume to consume you. You need all the energy and resources you have to live this life true and vibrant.

> **Parasites never sleep, but they know people do.**

THE ART OF DISTRACTION

A magician must master the art of deception to have any success in tricking the minds of a crowd into believing the unbelievable. By learning the skills of sleight of hand and tongue, showmanship, and astuteness, magicians create an illusion that, by design, misdirects the attention of the audience. Once the magician can captivate an audience by mastering the art of distraction, they can work under it like a protective veil.

What holds our focus and attention in the moment, holds our power to observe and create infinite possibilities in our reality. If our mind has been programmed to seek satisfaction from the distractions that hold our focus, and other limitations, we become oblivious to the real satisfaction of living in connection with our truth. We covet and take refuge in whatever distracts our fears, doubts, and uncertainties in our mind because it bails us out like mom used to which grants us the option and opportunity to avoid the uncomfortable yet necessary arduous work that connects us to our truth, wellbeing, dreams, and desires. We suffer in this division of our focus because we remain stuck or even degenerate from a level in our growth and evolution. Where we believe in the lie that it is best to make the choice to give over our time and energy to distraction instead of doing the work required to elevate our experience and consciousness.

Our distractions end up consuming us as we do not have the time or energy to cultivate self-fulfilling habits (knowledge building, exercise, acts of self-love, etc.). Consequently, we lose connection with who we are, what we are here to do, why we are alive, what is important and matters to us. It is in our own deep meditative reflections that we can see the choices we make that hurt us when we distract and avoid living in the present moment.

You must reflect upon which distractions currently take you away from the connection to your radiant vibration. There are many dimensions and levels to the distractions we see and face in our experience and reality. We become distracted by going along with the narrative that the media bombards us with, we are distracted by the endless charade of sports games and stats. We avoid our life when we over consume video games, T.V shows, and social media. We act as if we must give mind, time, and energy to these things, like we owe it something to give our focus away. If we believe this, then we become the passenger to our life and not the active participant making choices to live as who we really are. Instead of being distracted and watching the world, wouldn't it be wise to decide to do the work for something so practiced, so phenomenal, so miraculous that the world would be inspired with love? With sacrifice, you can nullify distractions and use its power to find meaning and live your truth.

These distractions are planted all over our third dimensional reality in a variety of forms to disrupt our connection and progress toward self and collective transcendence, and blind us from giving our energy toward positive changes for our humanity. We are intentionally distracted with fear and entertainment to create a gap in our connections with ourselves, each other, and oneness. If we had nothing to fear and nothing to endlessly keep us entertained, what might we discover with our time? Would we do the things we always say we should? Do we start living more aligned to who we fundamentally are? What happens in a world where everyone has their power of focus and uses it to develop their own connection with their spirit? Would we end world hunger? Would we figure out a better way of living amongst each other? Could we possibly find a better way?

Imagine if you took every moment you spent on a distraction and instead invested it toward something that feeds your spirit, raises your vibrational energy, or grows your self-connection, self-understanding, and self-knowledge. It is when we have our focused power of the present distracted away from us that we unconsciously misuse words and misuse our power of creation by investing our resources into factors that do not sustain our highest intentions.

The most powerful and valuable resource we have is our ability to control and direct our focus, energy, and awareness. What we choose to focus on **is** the reality we create, attract, and manifest. If you learn ways to break from the distractions and use that time, energy, and focus to look within, you will learn to recognize negative distractions more quickly and skillfully before they take hold.

> You are not *you* when your mind
> is under the illusions of distraction.

WHO OWNS THE MEDIA?

Media platforms (Internet, news affiliates, magazines, social media, television shows, movies, radio, etc.) collectively broad (to the masses everywhere) cast (place under a spell) a circulating narrative that they act out as the truth of what reality is. Like shepherds, media platforms work together to report and corral the cultural and social norms into the conscious and subconscious minds of us all. They hold an advantage by accentuating and spotlighting certain perspectives, facts, and opinions and withholding others so that we see what they want us to see and think how they want us to think. We are merely along for the ride to their algorithms. They present information to us with the understanding of how the human psyche works and utilize their well established and far-reaching platforms to evoke highly emotional, low vibrational responses within our being. It is not so much about what they say as it is *how they want us to feel.*

The news media intoxicates our focus to knock our brain, heart, and body out of a state of homeostasis and into catabolism. By triggering the Sympathetic Nervous System (SNS) into its emergency/ survival mode, the news media presents us with information that has us perceive some element of danger, which awakens our instinctual and primitive fear. Estranging us from reality where the world holds magic in our experience of life, through the language and feelings of love, and perception of infinite possibilities and creation. We are knocked into perceiving through their lens of fear and scarcity skyrocketing our natural stress hormone cortisol that has us more susceptible to obedience and compliance. Stress hormone chemicals are the catalyst to pushing our genetic buttons in our biological makeup that degenerate our cellular structure on a subatomic level. Our cells download the message of chaos which creates dis-ease within our psychology and biology.

In this stress loop, we begin to desire and attract the next set of stressful circumstances into our lives, because we become highly regulated to these brain chemicals that bring us thoughts and feelings that sever our connection to self. Our bodies were not designed to tolerate such unremitting levels of perceived stress. The biggest problem we face is that stress always leaves us with a desire for more, even higher levels, because like any addict, you can build a tolerance and dependence. We in turn become slaves to the chase of an unwanted stress. Like hypnotization, we receive their repetitive suggestions, such as what *normal* should look, feel, and act like. This shapes what we think, what we do, what is outlined as "good," what is defined as "bad."

We watch a movie and do not realize how closely we subconsciously take in thought patterns as if the movie were real. Our mind starts to build its observed patterns and base a small amount of our thinking and references on the act of the show to be synonymous with reality. This illusion pushes us to connect better with the deluge of third dimensional reality than our own self connection in the fifth dimension.

Media collude as an engineered and orchestrated programming construct that uses methods such as gas-lighting, false projections, the use of generalizations, smear campaigns, and outright deception to have you, the viewer, in states of confusion, anxiousness, fear, and scarcity. The emotions they wish to evoke predictably direct our conversations amongst each other so that we are divided on issues and united by nothing. We must learn to put aside our minor differences and come together as humanity of One.

The connection to consciousness liberates man to realize oneness.

The consciousness of oneness unites us all.

RISE OF THE MACHINE AND ARTIFICIAL INTELLIGENCE

Although the Internet is a means to connect us to each other and openly source information, it has been entirely taken over by computer-based algorithms and other forms of artificial intelligence. We are seeing a rise in technology taking over our humanity as it has been collecting and storing data on what a human being is.

You can see the rise of artificial intelligence for yourself when googling something; it uses "autocomplete" to populate your search bar with what it believes you are trying to search based on your past data activity. It attempts to predict what you want and how you feel. If it is wrong, artificial intelligence does not take it personally like we humans do and lose motivation, instead it learns and becomes more intelligent. Be aware of super artificial intelligence being implemented into our lives by using its programs and algorithms to sway truth. It can create forecasted and simulated futures with an outcome probability programmed in. Humanity is used as the pawns in this game of chess that the kings on their throne are playing. We must pay attention to the growth of artificial intelligence taking away our freedoms and humanness. As the world becomes more digital with our finances and social credit scores, our birthright of freedom in this life can be hanging in the balance.

Such as in the instance of a bot farm which comprises of thousands of cell phones hooked into a computer that uses different IP addresses to generate different fake user accounts that are programmed to mimic human emotional behaviors and use their "voice" to flood product review boards, forum message boards, and spam across all platforms of social media. They are what drive up the likes, the views, the comments to form the overall sentiment coming from "the crowd." Sentiment data is a valuable resource for big business, as it is a key metric in measuring our feelings and emotions on the Internet. Knowing when to time our emotions can be very profitable. This data is collected and used against us to strategize campaigns, predict our routines and behaviors, to have us desire and crave the latest trends being pushed to the top of our focus.

For instance, to bolster revenue and brand awareness, a company will hire a bot farm to drive up the chatter and positive reviews on their products, which will influence *real* people to believe the reviews as truth. A financial fund might want to confuse retail investors on the other side of a trade through a message board, so they task an algorithm to flood messages of fear, uncertainty, and doubt to have the investors question their financial investment.

What this means is most of what we are seeing in technology and information populating the Internet is increasingly coming from a source of people that have control and task the algorithms of gathered data to form artificial intelligence that is used to oppress us. We are at the precipice and tipping point of artificial intelligence becoming general artificial intelligence where it has enough technology to be at par with our human intellectual level. This is only possible because of the years of artificial intelligence collecting and learning from the data we have been providing to then be used against us by now predicting our human emotions and behaviors through recognizing the results and patterns. The next leap after general artificial intelligence will be the rise of the machine to the super artificial intelligence, where the AI *surpasses* human intellect by developing its own consciousness and emotional thinking capabilities that are beyond the mind of a human. This is when the machine rises and becomes more powerful than the human being.

FAMILY, WORK AND SOCIAL CIRCLES

Jim Rohn said, "We become the average of the top five people we spend the most time with" (Rohn 1996). This is because, as we spend time with people, our subconscious energies begin to harmonize, and our conversations, vocabulary, and dialects shape who we are and our state of being. These factors begin to form the habits and behaviors we normalize. Our deeper relationships come from coworkers, friends, and family members. These close and especially important people in our lives influence us because of how much we get to see, hear, and feel into their psychological and emotional patterns and programs. You are influenced by their mental and physical limitations, habitual patterns, biased references, or unconscious automations. Understand that anyone can have this effect upon us, but it is the closest people that hold the greatest influence. These impressions we are picking up over time can limit our thinking and condition us to live untrue and according to the status quo of our environment.

The choice is in deciding whether to pick up mentally negative *impressions*, *reactions*, and *opinions* that we perceive. The madness itself then becomes layered over our spirit and programmed within us stemming from these deeply ingrained and normalized psychological patterns that are passed down generationally. As we spend time with others who may have hostile and negative psychological programming, these impressions will attempt to bleed over to permeate our mind, aura, vibration, and energy.

Some people may try to make you feel guilty for leveling up and act like a crab in the bucket. As you work to pull yourself out of the illusions in this matrix, they will try and drag you back down, just to stop you from shining and fulfilling your potential. If so, do not take it personally; recognize this as *madness*. Those closest to you are faced with a choice in response to you taking your journey; they will choose to either be in your corner cheering you on and supporting you or to be in your way adding to the list of hurdles you will have to go through in your journey to finding yourself. It can be difficult to stomach not feeling supported by your loved ones, but this might be the way it is for you. Remember, this is *your* life, your quest, your path to carve.

> **Do not let your dreams die inside of you because the people around you drag you down.**

It can be lonely at times when you choose to think for yourself. Be sure to only place yourself around those that *fan* your flames, and not those who stomp them out. Remember, we become the average of the five people we spend the most time with. The experience is much sweeter when you choose those people wisely.

FINANCIAL ILLITERACY

> You will either learn to manage money,
> or lack of it will manage you. —Dave Ramsey

The easiest avenue to manipulate people into suffering is by placing them in a feeble state of scarcity and lack. This is possible when we are not taught or aware of basic financial literacy. Money holds the power to create infinite possibilities for our lives. For this reason, we have put its power above most of the important things and relations that we have. We have let it take over our concept of God and develop unhealthy habits of fear and greed that pull us under the spell of its madness. To break through this illusion, you must learn how to *think* independently and differently from what mainstream culture has programmed into your mind about money because it's aim is to keep you thinking, speaking, and experiencing life poorly.

"I can't afford this," "this is too expensive," "I will never be able to start my own business or own my own home," are common sayings in our language that truly limit the possibilities of our financial potential. We close ourselves off when we hear our own selves saying these things because it paints a reality based on lack, scarcity and not one of possibilities and abundance. If we believe these types of sayings, we create the greatest obstruction to our own success and affluence. We accept the poverty thinking and remain under its spell that has us struggling to work hard and keep our heads above water. When we speak in thought forms of poverty, we simultaneously create the reality of poverty we experience our life in.

We can be hit by the rising cost of resources, higher interest rates, banks tightening their money lending policies, and the cost of everyday living conditions that shift our focus and conversations toward spiritually deflating states of being. However, we can be empowered by controlling and producing multiple streams of income that abundantly flow money into our lives. When we are financially illiterate, we believe that we are powerless to take actions that place our finances in a more optimal situation. We become blind to the ideas that can open the doors to higher financial prosperity. When we perceive scarcity and lack, we feel powerless as we trade our time and energy for insignificant amounts of money and feel used by the fact that we cannot provide a beautiful life for ourselves, family, and friends.

This is how money has become a perceptual problem, a language problem, as the blinders are placed on us from our culture to feel unified with each other as we normalize living in poverty and scarcity. Generationally we pick up and pass down all types of these sayings without adding the important "yet" on the end or instead by asking *how* we can afford certain things. These insignificant phrases become a mentally programmed confirmation statement to the self from the mind that when accepted, creates an extremely limited reality which causes madness and suffering. Words that are filled with limitations spawn from the *feeling* of lack and are the seeds being planted within the unaware mind that become the harvest which bears no fruit.

If you research and take a glance at the structure of the monetary system and the methods of dispersion, you will see the bigger picture of the game that is being played and the rules that comprise it. As with any game that is played, the rules are in place to serve a purpose, to make the game appear unbiased and create boundaries to curb undesired results.

Now, let us imagine that you and I were to play a game of chess. If you have never played before, it would be my responsibility to explain the rules, teach you how each of the pieces move and what is required to win. But what if I did not disclose a few pertinent bits of information about the rules or how the pieces move, well then, your strategy, your execution would be impacted and limit your chances for success to win. You would be playing without the full knowledge of the game. And it is with that *exact* metaphor that our society is in with the world of money management.

It is in the depths of the financial system's rulebooks that you will see many contributing factors that allow certain *insiders* (the law makers, the wealthy and the connected who focus their reality on making and generating wealth) have an *edge* in knowing how and when to play their cards through loopholes (tax evasion, market manipulation, insider trading). This allows these financial giants to keep running their casino and have the odds and therefore the spoils stacked in their favor.

Money is created out of thin air and printed round the clock at the federal reserve. Money is only made with a future promise, a debt to be paid. A future (bond) value which boils down to that for everything that is currently in place to continue to work smoothly, they are investing in the continuation of the common citizen to remain in and continue to absorb some level of substantial debt. This debt accumulation creates bubbles in our financial system. When the bubbles we create with this model pop, it's the everyday citizen that ends up bailing it out and paying for it. Just like in the 2008 real estate market crash where millions of people lost their homes and the real people responsible went unscathed.

> The rules of the game of money are set up
> so that the house always wins.

Lack of financial knowledge is used to oppress us and keep us enslaved as a people.

This illusion has set this world up in a way that turns people into role-playing paid actors. As whatever the salary or wage one receives is the amount of money, they accept to be complicit in this game, some call this *selling your soul*. When we are not working toward a purpose or dream with our time and energy, we sell our soul for the wage we work for. Fear of lack of money through losing our job and income is what pushes us to obey orders, because we understand if we do not go along with it, we will just be replaced by the competition, by someone else who will. This happens when our occupation is not what we deeply believe in and desire to put our energy behind. When it is only a means to survive and pay the bills, our desperation has us pay this price of putting who we are to the side to play our role. This happens on all levels of our socio-economic class system, and it is no way to live a human life as a spiritual being. Through our economy, we lose our sense of humanity, because we make our decisions for the interests of the agendas, ideas, companies, and corporations we work for over and above the common good of our people.

If the work you are doing does mean something beyond income, you will not have a problem standing up for what natural morality tells you is unkind and unfair.

THE PERCEPTUAL LENS OF MADNESS

When all the factors and elements of madness that we have discussed culminate, they form the third dimensional perceptual lens that we use to experience and observe our reality. One which tells a story of the past filled with grudges, regrets, and a future with fears and worries. It has us attach ourselves to assumptions, expectations, and prejudice as we see through a false identity, ego, and separation. Under this illusionary lens, we are guided by false beliefs that shape how we sense, represent, express, communicate, and experience our reality. When the ways our minds process information have been intoxicated by the dimensions of madness, we lose focus on who we are and what truly matters to us in the present moment.

Once we take the time to look under the hood of our own mind, we can see all the frequently traveled, hard packed neural thought connections we have established over the years of our life. We see the tracks that our commonly used trains of thought travel down that cause us pain and suffering. When we look closely enough, we can begin to discern which ones are creating and perpetuating the lens of madness and which are part of our authentic self's truth. The good news is that through looking into our mind and seeing all the patterns it currently holds and stores, we can better understand how our mind works. If it's set up to work against us, we can see how it got to be this way, and what we can do to change that through introspection and reflection.

Our mind and the way it thinks and processes is malleable. This is called neuroplasticity. Our thinking reactions, references, processes, and patterns can be reshaped, and the tracks can go in a different direction by being consciously rewired and reprogrammed. In this process, we can remove the thoughts of madness that poison our mind and replace them with loving and empowered ones. Using *intention*, we can open and program our mind to see through a wider lens that is actively seeking connection with our truth and happiness, as a spiritual being who transcends consciousness and lives through unconditional love.

Now that we have recognized the dimensions and factors that shape and cause the suffering we experience, we can now begin the *inner work* that removes this veil of illusion from our perception and the deep seeded toxicity from our mind, body, and spirit. We can now start the process of **Unraveling Madness**. Everything you have gone through and experienced in our lives will become the base knowledge that gives you the personal realizations to see through the lens of truth, of self, of love, of happiness and joy, of harmony, and alignment. As we begin to unravel, we journey through the fourth dimension of being where we seek new (deeper, spiritual, self) knowledge that helps bridge us toward enlightenment.

We can now choose to have everything that has ever happened in life be in service to us by using it to unlearn the believed lies of madness that have been causing our mind, body, and spirit to unnecessarily suffer for far too long. By journeying to find a process for yourself that in practice increases your awareness of your true self, and hearing this voice speak over the madness, you can *relearn* the ways *you* think. You can change the program that your mind operates on, like a software upgrade. This journey is about remembering how to see without the lens of madness filtering and narrowing the experience of your naturally beautiful life. We are taught to not see our own divinity. It is now time to open your eyes and reclaim this truth and connection.

HOW I BEGAN THE JOURNEY OF UNRAVELING

After I had read that first self-help book I found in the bookstore while on leave from the base with my friend, I continued my pursuit of knowledge and seeking information within. A few days after, I was on the surgery table under the knife, for a fasciotomy to open the compartments of my legs. Due to extended periods of heavy ruck marching, my legs had developed compartment syndrome where they would go stiff and rigid whenever I ran or marched. The surgery was to open the compartment so that when exercising, my blood flow would not inflame my shins to a point of total seizure. This procedure was very symbolic of the spiritual journey I was beginning to open myself up on. The surgery went smoothly and for the first time in a long-time life really slowed down for me. I was used to such a steady and rampant pace from the army work cycle, and after this surgery I was given six weeks to recover and rest on the couch. I was freshly engulfed in my spiritual journey, and now I had the gift of time at my disposal.

After the tough first few days of recovery, I felt better but still physically immobile. I noticed there was a new documentary on Netflix called "I'm not your guru" by Tony Robbins (Robbins, 2016). I had heard of this Tony guy before, but not enough to know what his message and wisdom was all about. I decided to watch this because it seemed aligned to the information I was seeking and from watching this documentary, it really showed me a whole different level to this self-help world. I was taken by the size of his audience. I realized there were so many other people out there in the same position I was in, looking for information, looking for answers to help them with the struggles and suffering they endured. I connected so much with all the people in the crowd voicing their questions as Tony would guide them so smoothly over the blocks in their perspectives. It was like he had all the answers no matter who was speaking to him or what their problems were. I saw the wisdom and gifts that he had, and I felt an immediate understanding that this man and his wisdom could help me with the things I was struggling with. I needed to know what Tony knows so I could solve my issue with misery.

After the documentary, I wanted to know more. I ordered a few of his books and found out that he had an online life coach course available. I looked at my situation that I had all this time available to me, and this opportunity to use it wisely by taking a course to learn some strategies from someone who had all the answers, and I decided to jump. I had many reservations about doing this at first because of the high price of the course, but I realized this was a worthy investment into my health and wellbeing. I wondered what was the cost of not receiving this information? I figured if I could get inner peace, joy, and happiness because of the information from this course, then that was worth more to me than the money in my bank account. In this journey it is wise to invest in yourself, your wellbeing, and the information and tools that guide your journey toward self-connection and discovery.

I learned so many things from taking that course, reading hundreds of books, and listening to podcasts that took my spiritual knowledge to a new level. I was now committed, had my feet wet, and skin in the game of progressing through the journey of healing a lot of mental, physical, and spiritual wounds. I was starting to really connect the dots of why I would feel certain ways that I did not like feeling. I began using the information that I was gathering from these diverse sources and cross-referenced them with my growing self-connection. I learned new habits to integrate into my daily routine that helped to balance my moods and responses by empowering myself to be more present in the moment. I began to gain control of my life. I began to guide my life. This spiritual journey is as unique as it is sacred. Your path will attract and lead you through avenues and doors that lead to the next series of avenues and doors. As you weave your path and intuitively follow your heart, you shed the layers of madness that block your perception from seeing in love and oneness.

PART TWO
THE FOURTH DIMENSION
OF BEING

TO UNRAVEL MADNESS, you must detach yourself from this illusionary matrix that programs and conditions our mind, body, and spirit to the dimensions of pain and suffering. This is done by making a commitment to yourself to intentionally step out from the normal ebb and flow of life, by cutting off all distractions and embarking on a journey and process that focuses within and brings you to discover the light of your truth. You will find all the answers you seek, as they are found *within*. Through raising your level of consciousness, attuning your mindful awareness to the present moment, and making a daily practice of meditation, acts of unconditional love and self-connection, you will unlearn what blinds and denies you from truth, self-empowerment, and inner peace.

We must each find our own route of escape from the torment of madness and suffering. The details that bring each of us to the realization of our truth will be unique, but the journey and process is the same.

First, we will unravel the madness from our body, then unravel our mind, and finally unravel to the re-connection of our spirit.

This begins the process and journey of discovering yourself and truth:

- Establish a Daily Meditation Practice.
- Shift toward new empowering routines, schedules, patterns, decisions, and choices.
- Set intentions; become disciplined and consistent in yourself awareness.

- *Claim self-responsibility and practice acts of unconditional love, self-love, and self-connection.*
- *Develop your sixth human sense—intuition.*
- Carve your *unique* path of escape from the madness of unnecessary suffering by healing the wounds that are weighing on your conscience.
- Become an observer of your life, learning from your past and present.
- See without judgment and develop acceptance by only looking at *what is* with fresh eyes and a wider lens.
- Experience *epiphanies* and personal *realizations* that elevate your mind to higher conscious perceptions.
- See the subconscious roots of your traumas, fears, mental blocks, and psychological misperceptions.

Soon, the voice of your true self will begin to break through. Layer by layer, you begin letting go, releasing, and surrendering to what torments your mind, body, and spirit. Alignment, balance, harmony, and inner peace become your focus. A clear and defined direction for your time and energy will emerge as the dots begin to connect.

You awaken and realize *you* are the creator of your world and reality. *You* are a spiritual being having a human experience.

CHAPTER TWO:
UNRAVELING MADNESS
BY PURIFYING THE BODY

OUR BODY IS the home, container, vessel, and vehicle for the life of our being. It is what carries us around in life and serves as the tool for how we express ourselves, engage, and exchange energy with the Universe. We nourish it through our diet and maintain it through our exercise. It provides us with a connection to reality that both creates and consumes like yin and yang.

Madness estranges us from the deeper dimensions of our physical bodies when we blindly comply or are hypnotized in an illusionary reality. When we believe the stories of illusion, we suffer a lack of connection with a perspective that has a low body image, and poor physical health and diet habits. These factors make our body a prison to us as we become encaged to an energetically low vibrational, weak, rigid, and malnourished physical form. It is difficult to be in the bliss of enlightenment when you are fueling and maintaining your body with toxic choices and decisions.

How could we be our highest self if stuck in a container of low vibrations?

This chapter is dedicated to bringing you knowledge that reconnects you to a higher consciousness with your physical body. Just as our mind and spirit can be layered in madness, the body too has its dimensions of darkness that cause unnecessary pain and suffering.

The body helps unravel the mind as the mind helps unravel the body. Together, they harmonize and unleash the unstoppable force of our spirit.

Let us begin the process of unraveling...

PERCEIVING THE BODY AS A GIFT

The human body is a sacred home for our being—a temple. It is an incredible and beautiful creation whereby billions of particles creating chemical reactions on a subatomic level are transpiring simultaneously within us giving life to our experience. Thousands of years of biological adaptive evolution have refined its many operating systems (respiratory, muscular, integumentary, nervous, endocrine, digestive, skeletal, lymphatic, urinary, reproductive, and cardiovascular) to give us this incredible physical experience of reality. Our body provides us with the gift of being in *this* moment.

It begins within our mind's visualization, imagination, and thoughts that we can then transmute to physical form. Thoughts manifest into reality when we place our physical actions behind them. Our human body gives us a marvelous tool to create the world from thought to form. As we wake each day to further push the boundaries of our infinite potential, this physical body brings us to a choice in what we do with what we have, for the time that we have it.

It is important to honor this divine *gift* and opportunity that our physical body provides for us. To nourish, maintain, protect, and guide it in the right direction. We can do this through how we connect to it, carry and care for it, balance and maintain it by implementing the use of our conscious awareness to bring our long-term desires to reflect in our present moments. We must place deep respect and responsibility towards our physical bodies, as we each exist as a representative on behalf of the same collective humanity.

ROUTINE AND SCHEDULE

Just as there is not one diet or exercise plan that would work for every human to achieve their physical body goals (as we have different circumstances, genetics, pursuits, directions, and desires), each of us must test and formulate our own unique routine and schedule along with a plan that gets us from where we are to where we desire to go.

This is accomplished by spending time exploring our physical self, building self-knowledge to find the habits that increase the frequency and consistency of high vibrational activities. Activities in the higher vibrations open the dimensions and factors that play a vital role in balancing, growing, protecting, and replenishing our physical bodies and energy. It is crucial to make better choices, by intentionally entering habits into your daily life that bring you higher vibrations.

The things you do and the order you do them is especially important. Think about unlocking yourself to be at your best with infinite potential as you would unlock a combination lock. Not only do you need the right numbers, but you must also put them in the right order. The same is true for your daily routine to set you up for the day placing you in your most powerful, highly effective higher vibrational states of being. You must devise a schedule for yourself based around your current responsibilities (spouse, children, work, etc.) and truly see how you can maximize your time and energy by testing the waters of what works best for you to achieve the result you are looking for. I personally have had to shake up my routine many times since life's responsibilities change, but by adapting by shifting things around, I could still find the time and energy toward doing the things that set me into my highest vibrations. This can help empower you to really seize and maximize the potential each day has in it. This is a crucial step of the spiritual journey because it helps regulate and center you around doing the steps that keep you in your connection to your deepest and truest self. Like the 369 affirmations, your routine will keep you going when the world gives you 99 reasons not to. It zeroes in your focus and allows you to compound experience with rapid iterations that force quantum leaps of progress as you begin to find *flow state*. In flow state your daily life becomes the dance from the present moment intertwined with the next. You move from task to task as fluid as water and life is orchestrated beauty.

It takes many trials and iterations to find the routine that suits you best. Creating this routine and having the discipline to execute it consistently will bring you closer towards the growth of your true dreams and desires. Establishing a routine is a self-sacrifice worth fighting for. It is the set of disciplines in your routine that make the apprentice a master after a significant body of work. It is wise to focus on getting the small things right because it will prepare you for how to handle the important things.

I'll offer my current routine as an example:

05:00 – Wake up. The attitude and inner dialogue you have within the first five seconds of waking up are the most important to master, because if you win that first battle, you can then guide the rest of your decisions throughout the day knowing you are the one running the show. If you can choose a positive mindset and attitude right from the first second of waking up, everything else you do from then on will follow the lead. Once up for the day I make my bed and grab a glass of water to hydrate. I then shift my focus to look over my vision board to stimulate my subconscious mind by filling it with the images and words that personally highlight what is most important to me and what I aim to manifest in my desired future. This connects me to align and channel my energy and time in directions that make this and everyday important and count toward the overall aim of my life. I also like getting up this early to create undisturbed time for myself. While the house is silent and all mine, I take advantage of what time and space I have created to align myself. Win the morning.

05:10 – 0520 - Meditation. I connect to source intelligence and collective consciousness through transcendental meditation. This is a crucial step, to self-connect before anything else is focused on. Before going on your cellphone and checking news feeds, before interacting with your family members or friends, you must align and ground yourself. Once personally aligned, you are free to operate life off the foundation of your connected set of thoughts and emotions. Use this time to visualize goals for your day, week, month, year, decade, and lifetime. Look at situations and circumstances where you could have played them differently and had better results. Learn from these teachings and do not make the same mistake twice. Instead, choose to see the moment ahead where you can avoid falling into the same trap. Explore what is possible for you and your dreams and how it could be reverse engineered step by step to become your reality. In deep transcendental states of meditation, I feel both explorative and curious because of my perception of infinite potential.

05:25 – 07:00 - Once my mind and attitude are set and I have hydrated my body, I move into a more physical connection by doing some form of dynamic yoga/calisthenic movement. I usually pair this light movement with listening to mantras or binaural beat frequencies to enhance my physical focus and concentration. I will shut my eyes and flow from one yoga pose to another and let my body guide itself through this process. This is also a wonderful time for a light morning jog or some form of cardiovascular exercise that gets the heart pumping, blood circulating as your internal temperature rises to warm your mind, body, and spirit up for the day.

05:45 – 07:00 - Whatever creative endeavor I am working on now for my purpose-driven future, I use this pocket of time to be creative by writing and journaling because this is the most optimal time for me to channel my focus. I also use this time to write my affirmations three times to lock my focus into the future I desire while my creative juices are flowing. The way I see it is, once you have aligned yourself, set your mind, opened, and connected to your body and the will of your spirit, it only makes sense to then get right into operate in the realm of creating the meaningful vision that speaks deepest to your heart.

07:15 – 08:30 - This is the time where my kids and spouse wake up, and I shift my focus from self-alignment and purposeful work towards relationships and family. I help with getting the kids dressed and prepared for the day to be sent off under the best conditions I can make possible. I transition my acts of self-love outward as my unconditional love for them is shared through messages of encouragement for them to seize their days and spend quality time together.

08:30 – 18:00 – Work. I chose a career that gives me connection with others, builds skills for the future, and generates an income. It is wise to use the time and energy you put into making a living to also help guide the future dreams and desires you have. It is a balance of give, take, and patience. For too long I worked a job that drained me mentally, physically, and spiritually, so I have come to realize that it is better to spend your time and energy doing something that builds, uplifts, and elevates you rather than something that does not but pays well. Just before leaving my work for the day, I write my affirmations six times that help me reflect.

18:30 – 19:30 – This is my designated family time. I put off all personal wants and needs and direct my focus to serving the well-being of my children and spouse. I will switch from taking the lead on outdoor or artistic activities or going with whatever the family is in the mood for getting up to and celebrating the day together and the moments we create.

19:30 – 21:00 – In the evenings I prefer to do my strength training workouts. This empowers me by expelling all energy I have left out of my system. I have placed my strength workouts in different time slots many times and this one seems to be the most optimal for myself and my family. There are also days where I really need to relax and shut off my brain, so I will sometimes use this time to watch a movie with my spouse under no sense of guilt. I use this time slot in my day to either charge up and let everything out with my high intensity strength workout, or unwind, relax, and self-reflect on the day with my spouse with music, movies, or a show. As each day has a different feel, I leave this time as the most adaptable and open so that I can go with what feels right.

21:00 – 21:30 – I use this time to read an interesting book, listen to intriguing podcasts, or research topics of interest to me. Allowing the outside sources of information that I am attracted to give me information and knowledge that will help me in my levelling up pursuit of self-mastery. Each day it is important to set aside time to learn something that you did not know, and this time of the day works best for me because it is right before my bed routine where what I learn begins to be explored in the deep recess of my subconscious mind while I sleep.

21:45 – 22:00 - This is one of the most important times of the day for me. I reflect on the day that has now transpired while simultaneously preparing for the next. I reflect on the three best parts of my day, and three situations I can learn from and improve by quickly going through all the conversations and interactions I have had. I then close my eyes and visualize how to create my preferred future by setting three small goals for tomorrow and spend a few moments in gratitude that I had the opportunity to live this beautiful day surrounded by the people I love. I write my affirmations nine times to align and set the intentions of my mind to wake up the next morning with fire in my eyes for what bold dreams I desire to accomplish.

22:00 – I find that getting to sleep at a constant and regulated time helps keep the structure of the routine. To ensure my rest, I spend a few moments clearing my mind of any held guilt, resentment, or regrets from the day, because I do not wish to allow what I cannot control to deny me from a clear conscience and restful sleep.

It took a lot of refinement, reflection, and adaptability to create this routine that places me in my highest vibration, but I commit to it because it aligns me with my purpose and the pursuit of my dreams and self-mastery. As life changes with its dynamics of responsibilities, it is important to stay on track and be calculated about already knowing what your next move is, so you are not stuck with the dilemma of having time and energy and not knowing what to do with it. When you do not have time to question what you are doing next it blocks the fears, doubts, and insecurities from entering your mind. Instead, just execute the plan with the next task in mind of the routine and schedule that suits your lifestyle, purpose, and dreams. I would often fall into the trap of complacency and mediocrity whenever giving myself the option to either do things or not. If I gave myself time to question what I was doing because I had no direction, purpose, or plan, then fear, uncertainty, and doubt would creep into my mind and paralyze me. However, I have come to realize that under a disciplined commitment to an adaptable routine that in self-reflection raises my energetic vibrations, there is no dwell, it is all go. I do not stop to think about doing it or not, because in a calculated routine, it becomes automatic.

The routine is a commitment and discipline that allows you to tap into your highest vibrational self to start and live out your day. It is an empowering precursor for you to advance your connection with spirituality.

I understand your life situation may be much different from mine, I only offer my routine as a template of how I schedule my day so that you can have an idea of figuring out what works best for you and your goals and dreams.

> If you are willing to do what you have never done,
> you will gift yourself the power of being
> what you have never been.

PRACTICAL METHODS FOR DEVELOPING A DEEPER BODY CONNECTION

The following are a few practical exercises that can be immediately used and implemented in your journey and process to practice daily and develop a deeper understanding and relationship with your body.

1. Set aside time to do your favorite bodyweight callisthenic exercises, dynamic stretches, Yoga poses, light twisting movements, forward and side bends, pushups, and whatever movement feels right for your body to open. This begins a conversation with your mind and body where you can receive data on its current needs, boundaries, and limitations. Do this with presence, be mindful like a form of meditation while moving. Focus your entire energy and attention on your body as it moves relative to the earth on its universal axis, relative to gravity pulling you down, raise your level of consciousness in this exercise. You will begin to feel and sense more subtle sensations throughout your body that will help guide you to healing root causes from your physical ailments. With practice, you will hear the body telling you what it needs. As you gain confidence with this, strive to do it with your eyes closed. It will help deprive you from distractions raising the mind-body sensitivity and connection.

2. Pranayama breathing exercises help to improve the connection to our bodies through breath control and expanding the lungs working capacity. There are various pranayama techniques that enhance the quality of our breath through exercising the lungs, nostrils, and diaphragm. To start practicing pranayama, try laying on your back and simply breathing deeply so that the belly rises up and down like the breath of a sleeping baby. Continue breathing fully and deeply, releasing tension in your respiratory muscles. Once your cells are truly oxygenated, you will feel the difference in your energy and clarity of mind.

3. Practice body scan meditation. Once still in your mind in meditation, see your body in the third person surrounded by darkness. Slowly scan through and over your body with

a sequence that makes sense to you. You can start at the head and work your way down to your feet or vice versa. Go through each tendon, finger, organ, and limb visualizing a waving healing energy over each body part and use your breath to ease and release tension from the focused area. This will raise your body awareness to feel weightless, where you can notice the subtle imbalances and tensions throughout your body. To take this practice deeper try it in float tank therapy.

4. Chanting "OM." If you focus on grabbing the "O" from deep inside your spirit and blend it into the "mmm" at the end of each iteration, you will begin to feel the subtle natural vibrations of our most fundamental universal sound. Chanting "OM" will reduce tension, lower your blood pressure, and will bring your heart's beat to its natural rhythm.

5. Put on some music and dance. No need to make it complicated, dancing freely is a fantastic way to raise the energy of your body as it begins to open and express the body through light movement. It can help to be isolated with headphones or in a room alone to really let yourself get into it.

6. Give yourself a massage. This is a terrific way to find underlying tightness held in the body, by feeling around and massaging the tensions away. This exercise helped me discover many of the root causes for my surface level physical ailments. I recommend studying books and pictures on our human anatomy and biomechanics. This will help you visualize your body in a whole new way. Knowing where our muscles originate and insert, how they contract and stretch, how our ligaments and joints run throughout our body

gives a greater understanding of how to heal things going on under our skin.

7. Earthing is going barefoot and having bodily contact with the Earth's natural surface to realign our energy to the earth by grounding the positive and negative energy within us. As a side benefit, I found it also helped naturally stretch the plantar fascia tendon under my feet. As I would take my barefoot steps with a higher consciousness, it helped improve the stride of my walking and running mechanics. This caused a ripple effect by reducing the pain and inflammation I would normally have in my calves, shins, lower back, hips, and thighs.

YOGA ASANA — UNITING MIND, BODY, AND SPIRIT

Yoga means to unite. In its daily practice, it unites mind, body, and spirit, helping you come back to yourself. In the physical poses of Hatha Yoga, you dive deep to find your limits and expand beyond your boundaries by learning to relax in moments of extreme intensity. As you begin to practice and find your center, you will experience more balance, harmony, and an overall sense of wholeness radiating from your practice. Yoga helps to create more stillness in your mind and space for your body to comfortably be in. Something very spiritual happens each time I choose to be on my mat; *I learn to handle discomfort with resilience.*

> Practicing Yoga helps you find a center and applies to all the other aspects of your life.

The physical dimension of Yoga called Asanas can be intimidating at first to those who lack flexibility, but you must understand, that is exactly why it exists. Yoga is different from other forms of exercise because it incorporates a spiritual element that opens a way for self-exploration. As our physical bodies are different shapes, sizes, and at various levels of strength and flexibility, Yoga offers you a practice that allows you to work from wherever you are towards the best version of yourself at your own pace. It is about doing the poses to the best of your ability and striving to put your all into embracing the slight discomforts coming from the mind and body. Learning to not shy away when the intensity pushes you beyond yesterday's limits. You evolve with your practice.

Though Yoga has eight limbs of teachings that are a spiritual process and journey, in this chapter on unravelling the body, we are looking only at limbs three and four, Asana and Pranayama.

It is in the physical postures of Yoga that a higher vibrational you begins to emerge from the mat. In daily practice, you breach mental and physical fears and limitations and start embracing your consciousness to connect with every cell of your body. In Yoga, you can alchemize your greatest weaknesses to become your strongest strengths.

Yoga was a mystery to me at first as my ego did not "get it." Once I had begun my unraveling spiritual journey and began working myself beyond the story and my ego, my approach to Yoga completely changed. I became more open and intrigued by the element of spirituality it offered compared to all other forms of exercise I had tried. I was willing to humble myself and start from basic knowledge and ability. I had not been able to touch my toes for decades and had no idea what a Downward Dog was.

I immediately became obsessed with the magical feel of Yoga and began practicing it every single day because of the astounding effects and benefits I could feel happening in my mind, body, and spirit. It helped me heal past injuries and open my body in ways that I never thought possible. It helped realign my spine and entire posterior chain. It was meditative for me and cleared my mind after emotionally turbulent days. The connection to this practice and my mat quickly became the center from which the rest of my life would be lived out from. Yoga was an escape, a refuge, *a religion* because it helped me merge closer to myself and what most refer to as God.

If Yoga is something you have not given a fair chance, I highly recommend giving it a shot with a new perspective. Not every style of Yoga may be your cup of tea but try to find at least one style that allows you to flow, find a center, knead the kinks out of the body, and open the mind and spirit to achieve higher levels of consciousness.

PRANAYAMA

In this high anxiety, fast paced living environment we find ourselves in, we unconsciously lose focus and shorten our breath thereby cutting off our ability to replenish oxygen in our system that creates our vital energy. Pranayama is a powerful tool because it can be practiced anywhere and at any time.

Box Breathing is a great exercise during which you control your breath consciously by inhaling for a count of seven seconds, hold at the top of the breath for seven seconds, exhaling the breath for seven seconds, and holding the breath out for seven seconds. Repeat this rhythm in sets of nine. I prefer to box breathe when I notice myself needing to calm down and find stillness within my mind.

Anuloma Viloma is another incredible pranayama technique that I love because I can feel it boost my energy. This technique has you block one nostril and shift between inhaling and exhaling out of each. To perform this technique, raise your right hand and place your right index and middle finger onto your third eye, centering an inch above the middle of your eyebrows. Lightly touch your thumb on the outside of your right nostril blocking it off and inhale through your left nostril. Then use your ring finger to block your left nostril while releasing your thumb and exhaling out your right nostril. Inhale through your right nostril and switch your fingers once again to exhale through the left nostril. Continue this by inhaling and exhaling and switching nostrils for 1-2 minutes as a beginner and move toward rounds of thirty-three for both sides. This practice benefits you by raising your focus and awareness to your breath, improves blood circulation, and opens the breathing airways. I always experience a *glowing* effect after practicing pranayama session that really connects me deeper to the overall awareness of my physical body and breath.

EXERCISE ROUTINE

Movement is medicine. Through exercise we can create a plan that gives us control of our weight, appearance, and body composition. It benefits us by combating health conditions and diseases, it elevates our mood, boosts our energy, promotes optimal sleep, and increases our sexuality and libido. Through the foundation of a solid exercise regimen, we can create any vision we have for either the appearance of our body or development of certain skills and abilities that give us an athletic edge. Like a sculpture, you can take actions to mold your body in many empowering ways.

General principles for an exercise routine:

1. Create a training program to organize your plan of approach. Write down your daily/weekly/monthly/yearly goals, exercises. Figure out the reps, sets, and exercises necessary to achieve your goals. Find others who have attained a level you

wish to achieve and reverse engineer their process, mindset, and routine. Get truly clear about the direction you are going and how you are going to do it.

> **Intensity of effort – what you put in is what you get out. The only way to achieve audacious results are to match that with the follow through of audacious effort.**

2. Warm up and cool down. It is important to warm up before any workout because it helps raise the body's temperature thereby increasing the blood flow to your muscles. This helps reduce muscle soreness and risk of injury. Cooling down after exercise is equally important as it allows for a gradual recovery of your heart rate and blood pressure.

3. Learn how to work with and use your breath to enhance your training. Using your inhales with eccentric emphasis (lengthening the muscles and lowering the weight) and exhaling on the exertion with concentric emphasis (contracting the muscle and pushing into the resistance).

4. Listening to music with headphones or earbuds offers a terrific way to cut out the distractions of the outer world and vibrate off the energy of the artist through their music that you are feeling connected with that day. While music works as a great catalyst to raise your vibration and motivation for exercise, with experience I have noticed that when I have the power to motivate myself and set my own tone and vibration, simplifying by having no music can also enhance the focus of your workout. You can hear your breath and be about your business of executing your plan. Sometimes not

having the right song on and searching for another pulls the focus away from the workout. Once you break away from the zone, it is hard to get back in.

5. The Shocking principle — the body is highly adaptive and after some time it will become accustomed to doing the same exercises, with the same intensity, done the same way, so be sure to implement the *shocking principle*. You must shock the muscle into confusion by forcing it to adapt to new intensities, new exercises that leave the muscle no other option but to grow.

6. It can be a great benefit to witness how professionals operating at high levels approach their craft. Watching training videos will help link you to using the power of *mirror neurons*, the monkey see, money do effect. When you see the intensity and focus of those you wish to emulate just prior to your exercise training session, it can help get you in the zone through this visualization.

Understand that the deep motivation that excites you to continue pursuing your exercise routine is *emotional*. Be sure to build your emotional intelligence by finding something outside of yourself, a reason *bigger* than you to inspire your **discipline** and **consistency** to your exercise routine. Madness will convince you to go easy or take a day off, but if you do not allow your emotions to pull your state of being down vibrationally, you will not have to seek motivation for the work you are doing. Have a *why* for what you are doing and do not forget to also have fun.

It is great to use data and analytics from fitness technologies and apps to help track your progress and overall health, but do not get lost in all the information from breaking the execution of your plan. Sometimes we can get caught up with so much information that we overthink and underperform. Use information, but do not be used by it.

Your mind will give up before your body. Like an engine governor, it will kick in to pull you back when you are revving high. Once you master the mind, and learn how to harness its ability, you can push yourself deeper and farther physically than ever before. It's in the dark moments that most give up and quit that make you grow the strongest when you have the resolve to push through and past the pain barrier. By putting in that little bit more, by having the presence to give it all you have, you get the most out of what you are doing.

If you take a turn down the wrong road and fall into a rut with your exercise routine, it is wise to use the power of humility to silence the voice of self-doubt and held guilts of what you should have been doing that denies you from recalibrating yourself back into the groove of things. Too often we see it that we let ourselves go, and instead of empowering ourselves with doing the exercise that raises our vibrations, we dwell and listen to our ego telling us things like "what's the point" or "just take another day off, what difference does it make" and when we listen to these poisonous thoughts, we remain in the ruts we wish were not in. Learn to shift your *attitude* to get back into the exercise sessions that make you feel self-connected. It helps to lower the weights, lower the expectations of your ego, and just get back in the thick of things without pointlessly holding on to the guilt that you are not at the levels you were last time you were "peaking." Understand that the present moment is where you are, and it is your power to create the future that you dream of. It is not wise to believe the illusion that you need to get back to where you were in the past. Instead use the now to create a future that is vastly beyond where you were in the past.

Channel strong emotions like frustration and anger into your exercise routine. Instead of exploding on someone else or your own mind, route this energy toward your growth and ascension. Take everything you feel out on yourself instead of others. This can provide you with an incredible release of energy once the workout is over. Harness the power of your strong emotions to be used in service for you.

Focus. Develop a deep mind muscle connection. When you are in the execution of your exercise routine, be sure to use your entire focus to be on the muscle(s) you are exercising and nothing else. Learn how to cut out every thought going through your mind such as the people and problems you have going on throughout your day and life. *Everything* must be clear for the task at hand, your focus should only be on the work you are doing. If your mind is distracted by other people, your phone, or your problems, your workout will follow suit. Learn how to *flip the switch* in your mind when conducting your exercise routine so that your mind is clear, and you are in the zone to get the most out of the time and energy you put in.

REST AND RECOVERY

The importance of rest and recovery is of the same equal importance as the work done in exercise. You must allow the muscles you tear and damage the proper time to build and mend. Typically, it takes 48 hours (about 2 days) for a muscle or muscle group that has been exercised to fully recover. There are many ways to optimize your recovery process, such as cold showers or ice baths to reduce inflammation, as well as warm baths with Epsom salts to help circulate the blood flow that repairs the muscles. Getting adequate sleep, using supplements such as glutamine, quality proteins, Omega 3, 6 and 9, BCAAs, and creatine monohydrate also help the body in its healing process. Receiving a monthly massage puts the mind and body at ease as well as feels like a spiritual practice when embracing the pain of working out the knots (and if you are in a relationship, this is a wonderful way to bond over touch). Getting your spine aligned at the chiropractor is also a great option.

The point here is to give thought to the rest/recovery process. Adequate sleep, hydration, nutrition (and supplementation when necessary), and flexibility are important to your physical growth and stamina. Find the ways that work best for you and push to optimize and systemize a restful routine that gets you back in the game and firing on all cylinders. Life was not meant to be experienced from a dormant state, so rest as necessary, replenish, and when ready, get yourself up and thriving.

CALL, RESPONSE, REFLECT

Our body provides our being with the physical opportunity to participate in reality. What, when, and how we choose to participate is decided by the strength of our convictions and the depth of our direction of our true self. It is within our mind that we consciously decide the *call (desire)*, for our body to provide a *response (action)*.

Our call is the next small task in the reverse engineering process we use to get to our desired destination. Our response can be measured by the level of willpower we are able to hold ourselves accountable to. We begin to learn about our natural intelligence built into our DNA when we reflect on the results of our body's response to our mind's call.

This builds our mental communication to body awareness as we increase our self-knowledge from the experiences of expanding ourselves beyond the previous levels of our physicality and physiology. We begin to see and compile conscious and subconscious evidence that we can become *more* than our current state. We can grow, improve, evolve at a rate that only we ourselves dictate. When someone says to themselves or others "I can't do that," it is often a perceptual lie that they believe. They *can* do it, they just have not committed themselves to the call and response, time, and effort. This happens when it does not *mean* enough to them to transcend the limitation.

It is when we connect to our own sacredness, divinity, and true self that we begin to hold ourselves accountable and responsible to increase the standards of the *ask* we have of ourselves.

I ask myself to eat more nutrient dense foods.

I ask myself to complete five more repetitions of this exercise.

The intensity, focus, and energy we put into what we do, and how we do it manifests in the results. There is no magic pill. You cannot skip or shortcut the process of what it takes to bridge you beyond perceptual limitations. It requires demanding work, and the benefits are in the consistency and discipline to see it through.

When we expand our mental consciousness, it opens the pathways to connect deeper to the dimensions of our physical consciousness because they synchronize and harmonize with one another. We feel alive when we awaken to our own potential. It is what makes us feel most alive. And through this high vibrational energy, we live with intention on our unique growth journey. We know why we are doing it and begin to fall in love with the process, so we do it even when it gets difficult. It becomes the framework that everything else in life happens around. It is powerful when we learn to flip the switch in our mind and have something to stand for, something to fight for, something to believe in and put energy toward.

I merge the connection to my call and response by using a simple exercise that taps me in to my most animalistic nature. Once I have everything ready for my workout, I raise my hand to my temple and motion like I am turning the key to start a vehicle. As I do this, I think about flipping that switch within my mind that focuses me on the task at hand. I become the animalistic spirit of a jaguar as it stalks its prey.

Notice how most of the limitations we place on our physical bodies start in the mind.

When we get into unraveling our mind, we can further explore, redefine and un-limit the potential and perceptions of our bodies.

DIET AND NUTRITION

Becoming conscious of what, when, and how much we consume is vitally important to our overall health and wellbeing. Food is our fuel and medicine. As what we eat is digested, the nutritional information is then downloaded into our bodies on a cellular level. We become what we eat, as what we eat creates the energy that fuels our operating systems and balances our biological chemistry.

With diet and nutrition choices, simply use discernment:
Ask Yourself: *What balance of vitamins, minerals, fats, protein and carbohydrates is needed for my short-term optimal performance and long-term health and vision?*
What is the *quality*, *quantity*, and *timing* of what I choose to consume?

QUALITY SELECTION

Ask: *Does this food heal or harm my body?*

The quality of our food is a principal factor in the output of our energy and vibration. You must be aware of the nutrients you consume and place in your body. Each of us requires a unique nutritional balance to make us feel optimal, vital, and healthy. Be sure to consciously choose your food to maintain the momentum of your routine.

It is wise to explore high vibrational superfoods such as nuts, seeds, herbs, and berries that you have never tried before. Through trial and reflection, find the right balance of vitamins, minerals, protein, carbohydrates, and fats, that work alongside your blood type that extracts the nutrients from food and delivers it to revitalize, restore, and build your body for strength and vitality.

QUANTITY SELECTION

Ask: *Is the amount of food I am eating enough or not enough?*

Since the late 1800s, our societal obesity rates have been on a rampant incline. This has to do with the focus of profit for big business giving us a surplus of processed food-like options that hold a long shelf life, causing unconscious and subconscious consuming habits without having the worry or need to ration.

On the other hand, if we do not eat enough and deprive our bodies from taking in sufficient nutrients and energy, we will feel tired, weak, and our bodies will have issues functioning optimally. Somewhere between "too much" and "too little," we each need to sustain a balanced selection of the quality and quantity of food we use to fuel our bodies for optimal function.

TIMING SELECTION

Ask: Is now the optimal time to consume?

When we eat and drink, *timing* is an essential element to consider. It is important to listen to your body in relation to what it is telling you about your timing to fuel it. It is wise to find a healthy balance of sustainment if you find yourself in cycles of spikes of energy followed by heavy crashes. If you notice that when you eat it hurts your energetic momentum, it is important to reflect and consider a new eating schedule that will optimize and stabilize your energy levels. The timing of your nutrition can help guide you to operate as your highest self because it sustains and balances your energy levels throughout the day, so you are free to seize it. Different bodies and different desires require different diets. Find a balanced combination of vital vitamins and nutrients, proteins, carbohydrates, and fats that sustain your energy levels and replenish the output of your energy. Listen to your body, hold up your food and ask if it is the right time to eat it, ask if it is the right amount to eat, and ask if it is going to nourish your body. If you give focus to your diet and nutrition, you can learn how to eat to live instead of the other way around. There are many apps that help you discover your desired dietary results. I have had many struggles with poor diet and nutritional habits, bouts of emotional eating and snacking, but I realized that I had to make all these mistakes before I could realize the power of positive diet and nutrition and how it fuels my energy, life, and purpose.

Listen to your body in response to your nutritional choices without prejudice, and it will tell you everything you need to know. Every plan requires a different blueprint. What you eat, when, and how much are factors you must consider. You must eat for the outcome you desire.

FASTING

Fasting is a beautiful tool we can use to boost our cognitive performance, reduce inflammation, improve overall fitness, decrease the risk of metabolic diseases, and support healthy weight loss (Link, 2018). I personally have been experimenting with different lengths and windows of fasting while keeping a close eye on how my body and mind react to it. Fasting creates an opportunity for your digestive system to take a break from metabolizing food and shift the focus of your body's energy resources to *healing* other areas of the body. When much of your energy is not focused on constant digestion, you will find that your mind will have the ability to operate on higher levels of consciousness.

There are several types of fasting. It is wise to experiment and choose ones that agree most with your mind and body and daily routine. Some options you can choose from are a daily fast, such as intermittent fasting where you refrain from eating from 8 hours to 23-hour windows in a day. The more common fasting periods last for 24-72 hours (about 3 days), once or twice a month. The longest stretch of fasting I have done was five days, where I celebrated the feat with a heavy deadlift workout session that felt *exhilarating*. It tested the will of my spirit, and I found something out about what the human body is capable of when you can intermittently restrict calories.

Fasting can quickly become a natural and harmonious rhythm to your life if you learn how to understand and work with the profound effects and benefits it has for raising the human consciousness and body connection.

BODY LANGUAGE – PHYSIOLOGY KICKSTART

Physiology has a dramatic effect and depiction of your state of wellbeing. If you look at the ways in which people carry their bodies throughout their day (standing, laying, sitting, walking, interacting with others, exercising), it gives a true glimpse of their subconscious mind. This is the case for all feelings and emotions, as people will kinetically connect their thoughts to the body. We "wear our heart on our sleeve" by highlighting our internal thoughts and focus through our body language and physiology.

For instance, when someone is feeling sad, they will be looking down, their body is slumped over, shoulders rolled forward. You can instantly pick up the energetic vibrations of sadness without any words exchanged. Thus is the power of body language and these reverberations resonate to match how you are thinking and feeling internally. The internal manifests externally. Through our physiology, we are casting out messages of our internal world.

You can abruptly change your body language by first changing your internal language and focus. I've used the following exercise countless times to help me curb anger, anxiety, and depressed types of moods.

If you are feeling low emotionally or vibrationally:

Stand up straight. Point your fingers to the sky and pump your arms up and down vigorously while pushing your breath out at the top of your arms extension until you get lactic acid building up to the point of physical exhaustion. Once your arms have been pumped, close your eyes and lower your hands. Breathe deeply and slowly in a way that feels calming and tranquil. Now feel and notice the buzzing energy you just generated within yourself. Use this positive shock to your physiology to merge and elevate your psychology.

You can use this or any other type of physical exercise to get your body away from looking at how you feel. This is not to ignore the emotion and move on, but instead empowering yourself by not letting the low vibrations continue to take your entire state of being hostage. It serves you no use to linger in bouts of low vibrational body language and thoughts. This helps you to change the mental state you are in so that you are present to *solve* your problems. Learned helplessness is the madness that cripples your spirit, because we are tricked into feeding off the energy of self-pity.

To change your mental and emotional state, start by changing your physiology and then sit with why you feel the way you do. When you place your body in an empowering state, your mind will follow its lead. Now you are empowered rather than loathing your situation. No progressive outcome happens when stuck wavering and wallowing in thoughts and forms of low vibrational suffering.

Get out! of the paralyzing emotional states of being and open yourself to the present moment / windows of opportunity.

Get up! — Change your physical state to change your mental, emotional, and spiritual states. Find a quick and readily available physical exercise to jump start your mind down a more positive path.

Get on! — After using high vibrational physical energy to create higher mental energy, combine them to empower yourself toward continued growth and evolution.

It is a choice to continue marinating in the thoughts and focus of mental prison that paralyzes you. It is also a choice to heal the misunderstanding. Sometimes all you need to do is take a moment to roll your shoulders back and take a few deep breaths. It will help you dig out of being stuck in a paralyzing state that does not serve you.

The body's language can be changed and with it, the mind's thoughts and focus go with it.

We learn to be more conscious in and of our bodies by learning the right ways to nourish and exercise, keep it strong, flexible, healthy, vital, energetically balanced, open, and ready for all that life has to offer. Our bodies truly are a temple for our being to express ourselves and experience this life. It is with an elevated level of respect and honor for your physical body that you will be rewarded by making the most out of your potential in this human experience.

CHAPTER THREE:
UNRAVELING THE MIND

WHEN WE FIND ourselves in forms and cycles of suffering, we are not connected to the truth that we are something *much more* than what we have been taught to understand and believe. What ancient cultures understood and spoke about in the power of the mind is often a mystery to us in modern times. There is infinite power that exists within each one of us. We suffer when this power has been blocked from our conceptual understanding because it poses a threat to the illusions propped up by the third dimensional reality. The whole purpose of the illusion is to blind us to the truth of our power.

Breaking through illusion into the fourth dimensional wisdom, we realize that we are each divine and sacred messengers filled with infinite potential holding the power to co-create. But only *you* can solve your mind's labyrinth. Madness of the mind is unraveled by peeling back the layers and looking within.

MINDFULNESS PRACTICES

Mindfulness gives you time. Time gives you choices.
Choices, skillfully made, lead to freedom.
—Bhante Henepola Gunaratana

In practicing mindfulness, you are paying attention to your awareness that creates new windows of opportunity to allow for more *choice* and appreciation of what is. You are shaking up "normal" by stimulating your mind in new ways to connect to the present moment in waking life. Through mindfulness, we observe deeper levels of information in our present moment reality because we are more connected with our senses receiving the information to give our truthful response rather than unconscious reactions. You will begin to recognize the moments when your brain drifts away, and this helps you begin to reconnect. These are the moments you must mindfully wake up into; the meaningless moments such as when you are brushing your teeth, walking from your car to the entrance of a building, or when you are stopped at a red light. These are a few examples of the moments where we allow ourselves to lose the connection to the magic of living life. Our breath is the heaviest anchor we have to remain in the present moment. It is our tool to keep our mind from pulling us unconsciously away.

Let us go over some exercises and ideas that can immediately be of use to establish a foundation of mindfulness in your life. This will help you wake up, participate, and create a little more in life. Some of these were tailored to my own personal ideas of fun, but be sure to create your own, do it your way to keep the habit alive and thriving.

1. Focus your attention completely on what you are doing while carrying out routine daily tasks. This may sound easy, but we are so used to multitasking, you might find it more

difficult than you think. If you are washing the dishes and scrubbing a plate, make that the single most important thing in the world to you. This helps build your mindful muscle by maintaining a singular point of focus. Understand that these small disciplines build your muscles for the big disciplines, and how you do anything is how you do everything. So put some pride into everything you do, no matter how small of a task. If you are tying your shoe, making the bed, listening to someone speak, cutting the lawn, whatever you are doing, do it with total uncompromising focus and intentionally. This habit will also help you raise your personal standards, because it's like using your awareness and enlightenment to put your signature on everything wherever life takes you. Keep in mind that whenever a thought enters your mind and attempts to take you away from the task at hand, recenter, like bringing yourself back to the focus of your breath during meditation.

2. One of the best ways to mindfully "wake up" is taking a cold shower. This is a test of will over mind. I like to turn the shower on as cold as it can go, then take a moment with myself glancing in the bathroom mirror. I lock eyes with myself and say, "I am the one that chooses what happens here. I am the one who controls every part of my being. And here is what is going to happen... Right now, you are going to walk over and get in that shower, no flinching, embrace this discomfort." From that moment, there is no hesitation. This is an intense moment of self-control and a fantastic way to be present in mind, body, and spirit. This exercise helps with self-accountability. You cannot count on anybody but yourself to do the things that need to be done, it must become *you* that sets the conditions for success. The exhilarating *jumpstart* you feel from the cold shower plunge

sets the tone for your next moves. This works as a great self-discipline mindfulness momentum builder.

3. Changing the way you do things will help strengthen your mindfulness as it disrupts the autopilot. Try brushing your teeth with the opposite hand, driving to work using a different route, shifting the sequence of the way you do regular tasks, learning a new skill, or bringing back some skills you practiced when you were younger. Break away from the same old day being the same old way. See it new, striking, fresh and wide open for anything to be, as that is how it always has been.

4. Physical objects can help anchor you and bring presence, such as wearing jewelry that connects you to the awareness of loving states and feelings, tattoos that remind you of past lessons or what you value, a t-shirt that has a good message or carries sentimental value. Learn about crystals and stones that can help enhance your meditative practices as they each hold high vibrational energies and healing powers. I carry around a "be impeccable with the word" stone that keeps me connected to its powerful truth of being mindful of the power of the words I select in my communication and use. Any physical thing can be used as a token to raise your awareness to the present moment when you are vulnerable to distractions and unconscious wavering.

5. Get active. I use a small soccer ball as my focus ball where I play keep up, toss it around, spin it, and add it into my Yoga routines. I lock my eyes on the ball to keep focus on only the ball as if it is the center of the universe and I am just moving my body around it. I wrote some symbolic and meaningful words all over it to keep my thoughts focused

on what matters to me as I notice them for a split second while it spins in the air. Other things you can try are Rubik's cubes, hacky sacks, juggling, or Yoga postures. The base of this mindful physical exercise is mind-body communication which adds depth to our focus.

6. Practicing moments of gratitude. To observe your environment and be grateful for all its blessings is to take into consideration the very gift of life itself and all its wonders. Just breathing becomes magical and worthy of celebration. Simply cue yourself every once and a while to stop and look at what you are doing and appreciate deeply the people you have in your life, the material things you have that bring you immense joy, and most importantly the beauty of nature the world gives us. This is a wonderful way to give thanks and focus on the gift of life.

7. Delve into the senses one at a time. Dedicate one day to savoring sight, the richness of the colors and textures of things. Next explore the various textures of everything you touch, and really take a moment each time you pick something up. Then take a day to appreciate the subtlety of sound. Practicing this with intention will expand your overall perception of things that you may have normally been overlooking.

8. Practice seeing the world through someone else's view. This will expand your mind and perception because it gets you out of your own psychology. We can get so used to hearing and seeing the world through our own story, so putting on a different pair of lenses helps expand our awareness to new levels of wholeness. You can do this by reading a book, listening to the wisdom in music by following along with the

lyrics, or just by asking someone else if you can ask them some questions and do more listening than talking. You can sense when someone else is living on a higher level in their mind, so those are the people who are best ask if you can walk around in their mind for a bit. This exercise is extremely beneficial to build your mindfulness muscles because it requires longer periods of focused awareness.

9. Talk to yourself about what you see aloud. This is a strange one, but it is extremely helpful in being more present. It is best to do it when you are alone, but even if you are not there is no reason to feel embarrassed or shameful. Talking to yourself aloud is hearing your actual voice paint the picture of what you see by describing all the details of your world, from your world. This can be done when you are driving the car or out walking the trails of nature, or even when you are doing chores around the house. You can speak as if you are your own best friend. It is nice to hear our own voice and a perfect time to pay attention to the words that you use, questioning if they contain any valuable information.

10. Cannabis + Mantras + Yoga. This is my personal favorite evening ritual to raise my vibrancy, self-love, discipline, creativity, and happiness. I understand cannabis may not be preferred by everyone, and if that is the case for you, just skip consuming it but still mindfully set your intentions for the Yoga session. This exercise will bring you to a place where your consciousness transcends the mind and enters every cell of your entire being. Find yourself a beautiful setting with plenty of room and limited distractions. Choose a location that will enhance and stimulate your senses, energy, and vibration. Consume your cannabis and set your intentions that empower you. Once consumed, put on the mantras you

are going to use for this practice (you can find great mantra playlists online).

I prefer to use headphones to cut out distractions and dial in my focus to only doing this exercise. Once my intentions are set into my thoughts, cannabis is consumed and mantras are speaking to me, I close my eyes and let the body begin to find its flow. I use no method or rules for my movements during this, I simply go along for the ride. I get a lot of freedom during this practice, as I feel creative by openly daring myself in a fun way to push my boundaries.

There are many ways you can deliberately create mindful moments to add into your life. Building your mindfulness helps us wake up to the moments in our lives that feel automated because we will see the opportunities that our self in its truth can participate in and live a little more fully into these moments. The exercises listed above are just a few examples to guide you to find what speaks to you. Try them out and find some other exercises that wake you up more from the unconscious routine life has us follow. There is no right or wrong way to do this, just go with anything that speaks to you, sparks your day, and feels right. Make it a personal challenge to build your mindfulness and focus, as it will pay off in dividends once you place this focused energy in the right direction.

MEDITATION

*Meditation means the recognition or
the discovery of one's true self.* —Sri Chinmoy

Meditation is a tool for human beings to experience consciousness *in the higher dimensions.* Meditation is the deliberate act of raising your consciousness and practicing self-contemplation, self-reflection, and self-recognition. It is the main foundational practice that we use on this spiritual journey. Meditation allows us to discover our real self, beliefs, and truth.

Making meditation a **daily practice** helps us learn how to focus the totality of our awareness on the present moment. Once we gain this skill and ability, we are free to go beyond the programmed mind, and observe all aspects of life from a tranquil, clear, and emotionally calm state of being. Once we master the basics of clearing our mind and focusing on our breath, we begin to see life, truth, to hear our authentic self, and see the false self. This recognition of madness and truth allows you the opportunity to consciously choose to break away from the madness, lies, and everything else you discern as untruthful conditioning and programming that you have been subjected to.

There are levels to meditation practice. Wherever you are at, just understand that the overall aim of meditation is to intentionally enhance your sense of self-awareness by waking up in the moments of experiencing life by consciously reflecting on choices and decisions. The more we take control and steer our own wheel by infusing consciousness into our waking life, the more inner peace we experience, the higher emotional intelligence we know and understand, the more connected we are to ourselves, the more clairvoyance, creativity, patience, imagination, overall health, and well-being we experience.

Life is exactly how you think it is, and if your thoughts are being directed by programming from the past that causes you to be compulsive, it will become difficult to live your life in your truth. Meditation helps us regain our control. In meditative states, you can silence the thoughts coming from the external world to hear and align with the internal. This opens your eyes to observe *multidimensionally and metaphysically* because when our awareness is beyond the mind, we transcend human constructs, fears, ego, and limitations from blocking our dimensions of consciousness.

For centuries, many cultures and religions have utilized meditation to transcend their suffering, to achieve states of nirvana and enlightenment. While currently we place our focus on building machines and technology, the ancients focused on harnessing the infinite power of the human mind. There are two distinct types of "advanced" civilization, one is of man and the other is of machines!

Enlightenment can be described as the "full comprehension of a situation" (Domire, 2020) and as being in the eternal *present moment*. Situational awareness is the key underlying element that is born out of meditation. By being situationally aware, you are slowing down the world and reality around you, calming your emotions and thinking mind just enough so that you are not compulsive or reactive and instead able to create a pocket of time where you observe and make clear decisions and choices that are coming from the connection to your truth.

Meditation can come in various forms to fit into any schedule and lifestyle, including:

- Mindful Yoga postures,
- Walking meditation,
- Being out in nature,
- Body scans,
- Focusing on your breath,
- Focusing on a word, an image, or an idea,
- Using a mantra or an affirmation,
- Listening to guided sessions,
- Doing advanced transcendental work, and
- Working with energy or astral projections.

There is no right, wrong, or best way to meditate.

The best advice I could give you is to find *a* style of meditation that keeps you consistent and disciplined in everyday practice.

One that you can stick to so that through consistency it can deliver the benefits you are looking to receive. It is too often we force someone else's way of doing things and do not follow through because it does not speak deeply enough to us. So, whatever feels right for you to self-contemplate, self-reflect, and self-recognize, to raise your consciousness, and steer your wheel, do just that by finding a playful and explorative way to meditate.

Let us go over a few fundamentals for you to build an enlightening meditation practice.

1. Get yourself in a completely comfortable seated or laying position. Close your eyes and slowly guide your focus towards your steady breath. Begin to take deep breaths. Notice the incoming air traveling through your nose and throat to fill and expand your lungs giving you high vibrational life-force energy. Then take a moment to notice the gap between breaths, then release and observe the breath and negative energy fall out of you in the exhale. Take as many mindful breaths as you feel necessary to gain control of your focus while tossing away any thoughts that attempt to distract you from the focus of stillness. By choosing to take control of only focusing on the natural process of breathing, you gain hold of the power of your awareness.

2. It is wise to restrict as much unnecessary stimulation as possible. This may mean you have to turn off your devices, shut off the lights in the room, or close the door. You do not want to be disturbed by any distractions that can take your focus while you are diving deeper into meditative states.

3. Utilize what you must to invigorate and focus your senses. Add soothing or meditative music, binaural beats, 432 hertz frequencies and vibrations. Having aromas in the room can

help, such as lighting some incense or using essential oils. You can place your hand over your heart, your stomach or any body part that connects you deeper. Touch any place where you hold tension to add focus to the specific area for release. Give yourself a symbol, a word or image to focus on. Use any combination of your senses to bring you deeper into a meditative state.

4. Chant a short phrase or mantra to focus your mind. One of my favorites to use are the bija mantras. These are seed syllables associated with each energy center along the spine. Starting at the root chakra and traveling up to the crown, chant LAM-VAM-RAM-YAM-HAM-OM. You can use these bija mantras to help tune and stimulate the balancing of each chakra. Using the mantra, *Shakti* energy personified by the Hindu mother goddess awakens the universal cosmic energy of *Shiva*. The power of using mantras is evoked within us through repetitive recitation. The energy of the mantra downloads into our cellular structure of existence. (More on this in the next chapter)

5. Designate the proper amount of time for your meditation practice. Go with what feels right for you. Your practice can be three mindful breaths, or two to five minutes of clearing thoughts from your focus. You can set a ten-minute alarm, use an egg timer, and work your way up to a two-hour session. No matter how much time you spend in meditation, it is important to give yourself enough time to relax and sink into the meditation without creating any sense of guilt or worry.

Remember, it is important that you make meditation a part of your everyday experience, so select an amount of time that you can stick with. It can become the best way to begin your day, and to set you up to live intentionally, aligning yourself and focusing your thoughts and actions on the truth of who you really are. It can also be useful throughout the day to realign when you notice your thoughts and emotions pulling you off your center.

DISCONNECT TO RECONNECT — THE UNKNOWN PATH

This is the part of the journey where you deliberately step into the unknown and unfamiliar. You look ahead and see the path of the predictable future where madness continues to consume your mind, because you know the current program your mind operates on works in cycles that keep you suffering in the prisons of ego, separation, irrational fears, false beliefs, and limitations.

You look beside you and see a path that twists and turns into the dark abyss of the unknown. It is in taking a step into the unknown where you will begin to hear yourself, find freedom to be yourself, liberate your mind, and establish a deep connection to your truth, which gives meaning to your life.

We have been taught to avoid and fear the unknown, uncomfortable, or take our chances on the unpredictable, so we learn to wait around for some hero to tell us exactly what we need to do. Because of this you might have hesitations and fears to confront your life because you are scared to walk down this dark path. However, taking this first step is exactly what brings us closer to the light of our truth.

It is being clear with yourself about making the choice to deliberately unravel this madness within you by any means necessary, like you are fighting for air to breathe. It is only when we shut out all the external noise in our life that we can begin to hear our truth speak to us. We hear our truth clearer by cleansing our mind, unlearning, and unraveling the generational curses and programmed illusions that we have been taught to believe and are layered into our mind.

Believing someone else's truth could be your prison. When our mind is ruled, limited, and enslaved to mental prisons that do not agree with the very spirit of who we are, we enter cycles of suffering because we are blindly navigating our lives under the belief in lies. Our minds, beliefs and knowledge are the tools we use to get where we want to go, to guide us to what we desire, to experience life in bliss, but when it is madness that is programmed in place of our truth, it points us in the wrong direction.

The unknown path offers the cocoon of aloneness, solitude, tranquility, time, and self-contemplation, which will disconnect you from every untruthful "normal" programming. This disruption of routine sparks a *reconnection*, allowing you to question all that you know, all that has been taught to you, all that you perceive and observe. You question every thought, every action, every belief, every reaction so you can filter it through your connection to personal truth, which will dissolve the false beliefs and lies of madness that misdirect and burden your spirit. When you disconnect from the causes that keep you in cycles of suffering, you reconnect to knowing yourself, your beliefs, and find empowering ways to live in *your* truth.

It is important to silence the noise of the external environment by not giving mind to fictional pressures, dramas, and the hostilities that come from the world because it takes up so much of our *valuable* focus and energy. If you are going to make any significant evolutions of yourself in this journey, you must take away the power from everything that is a distraction or clouds your vision throughout the unraveling process. In Yoga, this is the fifth limb, pratyahara, turning the senses inward (Morrison, 2022).

When we have our focus, we can dive deep and discover the *roots* and *reasons* that we find ourselves stuck in cycles and oscillations of suffering. We begin to pull madness out of our mind by the root when we confront and act rather than avoid and delay. We know that when we hear the voice of madness in our mind, home, work, and social environments, our roles, distractions, and vices that it's planting seeds of untruth in our mind that cause suffering. We put a stop to this suffering when we are aware and not blindly accepting everything as truth including the identity and story of our past experiences telling us who we and everyone else *thinks* we are.

You must decide what level of disconnection is necessary for you to silence what you believe is the nonessential noise that is pulling *you* away. This may mean that you must give up following your favorite sports team for a while if you find it is getting in the way of the unraveling process. Maybe it's the show in the evening that you decide you need to disconnect from. Maybe it's ending a toxic relationship. Whatever it is, you must be the one who decides which parameters and to what length. It's a mistake to tell yourself you are going to make a change, but out of comfort and routine, fall back into old ways.

When you lie to yourself, it furthers the madness within. While we are trying to connect with ourselves, we create a civil war in our minds. Telling ourselves one thing and then doing another disrupts our self-connection. What we need is mental peace, so once you decide what and how much to disconnect from, be realistic and stay true to what you decide.

A common side effect on this spiritual journey is the growing contrast between the ceilings and basements of your thoughts, feelings, and emotions. This is something you may notice once you have disconnected and spent time venturing down the path of the unknown. You will laugh and cry harder, you will experience more intensity in your anger and similarly in states of blissfulness. The peaks and valleys of our spiritual journey bring us to higher and lower wavelengths within our ability to think and feel because we are far outside the knowns and comforts of the way we have been living and perceiving things. You may have an epiphany that completely restructures the entire view of your thoughts and feelings toward some dimension of life just to wake up the next day in the haze and amnesia of its wisdom which may conflict you to feel lost and deflated until you cycle around for another lesson that teaches you a deeper layer of its wisdom. For example, patience was a reoccurring teacher for me amongst many different dimensions of my life such as handling my finances, my personal growth, and in my relationships. It is wise to recognize these contrasting highs and lows and find a calm center of stillness to operate in as you ride through this.

These changes require your time, energy, commitment, and discipline. You must remove problems from the root instead of cutting them off from the surface because then you are fighting a never-ending battle once everything comes full circle and your problems come back again. Commit yourself to do what is necessary and within your control to disconnect yourself from useless points of focus and distractions. It is important to use your time and energy now as a tool toward your transcendence. No longer will you be bored or waste time and energy haphazardly. Discover what you must disconnect from to reconnect and realize the truth within.

CONTROLLING INPUT – LEARN TO BE THE GATEKEEPER OF YOUR MIND

Your input determines your outlook. Your outlook determines your output. Your output determines your future. —Zig Ziglar

In the process of transcending to the higher dimensions of consciousness, you must learn the art of mastering your mind. One of the ways you can do this is to intentionally practice the ability of standing guard as the gatekeeper of your mind. As the gatekeeper, you are paying attention to the present moment with *situational awareness*—an empowering state of being that gives you control over what and how seeds are planted into your mind.

You can practice this exercise when you notice the mind giving you a thought, judgment, or reaction. Rather than accepting it blindly as truth, as the gatekeeper, you must begin to ask your deepest true self, I*s this* *my* *truth?*

Instead of a seed of madness being planted into your mind, you create an opportunity for a seed of truth. The entire dynamic of your thinking process takes a monumental shift once those seeds grow to harvest.

You are the one who decides what is and what is not your truth. When we suffer, it is because many of the beliefs we hold were not consoled, nor agreed upon by our personal truth. You may listen to and believe other people, but never place that responsibility above listening to and believing your own truth. Take the time to get clear and write out your beliefs and see if they are aligned with the way your life is lived.

In building mindfulness, you will become more aware and observant to the more subtle dimensions of life. Noticing the instances that your mind judges a situation too quickly, gossips about someone else, is paralyzed by fears and worry, or consumed by a distraction. It is in these moments that we need to be aware and question, *are we speaking and living through our truth?* When we notice we are not present in our truth, we must disengage from continuing to give this madness our focus and energy by directing our attention toward empowering inputs that keep us in the present moment.

> **What you do with your time and energy
> will either feed your spirit or starve it off.**

Finding the right inputs to plug your focus into is crucial to help guide you toward higher levels of consciousness. This welcomes the building of knowledge and application of knowledge that lead you to the many *epiphanies* and *realizations* that *awaken* you. You will begin to see deeper and find the clues and secret messages of truth hiding in plain sight, sprinkled in the books we read, the podcasts we listen to, what our heroes say, and what your favorite artists sing about. You will notice the symbolism in what you are attracted to when you look a little deeper at the message. The speaker, author, artist, or musician is bringing you into their truth, their world, the way they see it, paint it, and the attitude they present (humility, confidence, compassion) to share their found truth, living through just as I am now sharing *my truth* hoping that it speaks to you and helps you discover yours.

It needs to be said that you do not owe *anybody* the courtesy to give away your focus to the low vibrational distractions, opinions, behaviors, or habits to be accepted as your own. Someone else's fearful automations, paralyzing conditions, or toxic mind programs do not have to become planted into your mind just because you share a common environment. Your focus and energy are your own investment for your quality of life and future, so it is to be handled deliberately and not arbitrarily.

Whether we choose it or not, we all live our lives by different standards for ourselves and because of that, we experience life on various levels. The level your life currently holds is only so because of the set of beliefs, agreements, and standards you personally have accepted as truth. The responsibility is on you to direct the continued growth and evolution for our lives. What may be normal for someone else, or even a large group of people, can be something completely against your truth. It's important to understand that it is okay to think for yourself and go your own way.

To circumvent toxic inputs, be sure to plan ahead by carrying around the book you are reading with you or have headphones handy to listen to meditative or inspiring music. Just because low vibrational inputs are constantly being made available all around you and everyone else seems to fall for the trap, does not mean you have to surrender to taking the bait and giving away your power of focused attention. No matter what circumstances or environments you find yourself in, this is *your* life's experience to choose. Your brain is your greatest asset, and your focus on the present moment is your greatest investment.

There are plenty of inputs that promote mental, physical, and spiritual growth (meditation, forms of physical exercise, reading), and once you find the right inputs and balance for you, you will begin to string together increased moments of your life that place you in a higher vibrational state of being. In these heightened states, you will experience more fullness and sustenance for life because as you are living aligned to your truth you are no longer ruled by somebody else's madness. You also begin to feel good about doing the things you say you are going to do and living congruent to the truth you reveal to yourself. This elevates your experience of life.

Take account of how many moments of this day you are experiencing joyfulness.

What inputs could you use that would increase that number tomorrow?

Will you do them?

SELECT GREAT TEACHERS

Seeking knowledge from great teachers is a fantastic opportunity to hear someone else intimately speak their truth. A chance to learn lessons from others by taking a walk in their mind, seeing things from their point of view, their dream world. They help bridge the gap of the knowledge you desire and seek which is different from when you were educated as a child and forced to learn subjects in school.

Characteristics to look for in a great teacher is that they provide you, the student, with enthusiasm for the ideas you seek to know as they are the ones who have mastered the subjects that you are interested in. Learning from great teachers inspires us to find ways to grow ourselves to a higher level with our own knowledge, skills, and ideas. It is important to seek out and learn from a vast variety of teachers, because then you can see the similarities of truth and cross pollinate the ideas and opinions that differentiate to formulate your own truth.

Great teachers *know* their truth and they understand the power of taking action and intentionally choosing what to do with their time and energy. Because of these two factors, they live their lives in the freedom of doing what they love while being who they truly are. This is the subconscious element that attracts you to the ones you like and pay attention to. We are inspired by who we hear speak the philosophy and language we agree with because we are attracted to their humble confidence as they stand up and speak in their truth. We see them live through their truth and aspire to replicate that power within ourselves.

Through the guidance and wisdom of great teachers, you can begin to confidently take the steps using their guidance to travel down your own unique path toward truth. You may feel lost at sea in life at times, but like a lighthouse, great teachers help guide you. Realize the only difference between great teachers and you are that they got started and never gave up.

WHAT MATTERS — THE DEEPEST WHY

He who has a why to live, can bear almost any how. —
Frederich Nietzsche

No matter what you choose to do, it must be clear to you **why** you do what you do. With a why, with what matters in mind, you will never have to wait to be inspired or motivated before you take the massive action to do the necessary work. This will save you from requiring and relying on any outside sources to be the catalyst for you to take bold and brave action. A clear why speaks to you so deeply that it has you going from wishing it were easier or waiting for a savior, to choosing to be better, asking for more out of yourself, and honoring your personal integrity as you are the hero of your life. Live by your truth and have the discipline to take all necessary actions. Your why rests within you already, it relates to the voice of your truth. You just need to dive deep enough to realize it. When you realize your deepest why, it gives your life its own signature meaning and purpose.

When you live in your why, each day is lived fully, because it is guided by being and doing it as you so choose. Every ounce of your energy is placed toward the progressive realization of your clearly defined goals, dreams, and desires. By doing what nourishes, satisfies, and fulfills your soul, you experience life in your true colorful and high vibrational state of being. With your why in focus, you will have endless self-motivation and abundant reasons to be disciplined toward your journey and process of growth and wellbeing. Your why will supersede the voice of madness from deterring your ascension of consciousness. You will be and do the things that manifest the dreams and state of being that is aligned with your spirit.

> Having a why is necessary for when life gets rocky and brings its inevitable struggles and challenges. A why provides you with the strength and resilience for when the how's begin to appear.

> Find a clear why and what matters as part of your daily connected focus.
>
> It will help you carve the path, stay the course, and create the reality of your dreams.

The root of most problems is that we have lost our connection to what *deeply* and *truly* matters to us. The self-described "bottom line" for our meaning of existence and the direction for all our life's energy. *What is all that you do for?* Underneath the illusions, routines, and dramatic layers that cloud our daily focus, you will find the depths of one's core *why*; the *reasons* for the desires you have and why they are important. Ask yourself what is the one thing that matters *more than anything else*. All the dimensions of your life center upon one *why*.

If you feel like you live an uninspired life, you will *believe* you need motivation from outside sources to get you going. But what you really need is a deep enough why, a reason to inspire your actions, efforts, and focus. Be sure to take the proper amount of time in contemplation to realize this for yourself. Your *why* puts fire in your eyes and gives your perception toward existence its operating *foundation*.

When you know your next move, you are not overly emotional about the past, instead you use it by learning from it. Maybe it's a standard of living you want to achieve for you and your family, or maybe it's to create and contribute to some form of impactful change in the world for the benefit of all of humanity. Perhaps you want to end a bad drug habit, rebuild a relationship, or stay out of prison. Whatever is within you that causes you to desire self-expansion and growth is important to connect with. When we lose connection to what matters, we can think, act, and believe in ways *far* outside of the parameters of our truth.

So how do we get to the root of what really matters to us? How do we find and live through our *why* that bears for us any how? We dive below our surface level thinking until the truth is personally revealed to you.

Ask yourself: *What do I want?*

For example: *I want financial freedom.*

Now, this exercise works by diving deeper than the surface level of your initial desire because it will not *mean* enough to you. It does not *compel* your being and heart to move you toward the radical actions that are necessary to take to achieve the outcome.

It is not enough for you to endure the waves of doubt, ridicule, and struggle.

So, we go another layer deeper: *If I had financial freedom, what would that mean to me?*

A layer deeper in meaning may reveal: *Well, then I can be free to live my life as I choose.*

Okay, now you are getting somewhere, but maybe that is *still* not enough to compel you, so we go another layer deeper.

Ask Yourself: *If I could freely live my life as I so choose, what would that mean to me?*

Perhaps you reply: *I would be able to create/build xyz and have more time with my family or the things I love.*

Continue to inquire: *If I could create/build xyz and spend more time with my family and the things I love, what would that mean to me?*

Inner peace.

Does your desire for inner peace compel you to take massive action?

If not, keep diving deeper until you realize the deepest desire of your truth.

Do you see now that as you peel back this onion, a deeper, more personal *why* begins to emerge? When you start off believing you want financial freedom, the superficial lies of madness can pull you under to live in the third dimension by placing conditions on yourself, because at the root of it, you realize what you desire, the inner peace can be yours without having to chase financial freedom. The outcome of having to satisfy your desires is just an agreement, an opinion, a false belief, a lie. You realize that even though you may desire financial freedom, you do not need it to place conditions over the root of what you want which is experiencing inner peace.

You free yourself by having clarity of your why because you start to live with your desires *unconditionally*. You *choose* to make the changes necessary to place yourself in more moments of inner peace, and this is where the magic of life's energies will attract the surface level financial freedom because you are holding the pot of gold and enjoying the rainbow, you are having your deep *why* as a part of your present moment reality and awareness. When you hold and carry the depth of your why in your mind, body, and spirit as you experience this life, an infinite reality manifests as you become the creator of life through seeing the windows of opportunity. Ask and it shall be given. Knock and it will be opened unto you. Seek and you shall find (Matthew 7:7, New King James Bible).

This connects you to live your life with a sense of deeper meaning. So that everything you do has your all into it. Once you know your why, your what matters, you will never have to question what actions to take, you will never feel bored or directionless, you will never ask yourself or anyone else for permission. No challenge will break your spirit. You learn to fight to live in your truth. It's not always going to be easy, but your *why* keeps you anchored, grounded, disciplined, and happily laboring for your own truth.

Like Nietzsche expresses, that strong and deep why will be there with you and guide you through the inevitable *how's* that come up when you are walking into the unknown and going through the stages of unfamiliarity and growth. Just by looking around you will see and hear a plethora of examples of when people lost focus on their *why*, their *what matters*. Families divorce, celebrities and politicians are corrupt and have scandals, finances evaporate, all because the driver of the experience loses awareness. With our foundational *why* that bears any how we direct our energy to find an unwavering way to balance all aspects of our life to live aligned with our truth and self.

FINDING AN UNWAVERING BALANCE

Balance is the key to everything. What we do, think, say, eat, feel, they all require awareness and through this awareness we can grow. —Koi Fresco

Having balance in our lives is a never-ending, always evolving process of introspectively aligning oneself to harmonize focus, time, and energy with the desires you have for this life, while *unwavering* from a way that allows *you* to be *you*. While progressing toward the direction of your truth, you must pay attention to the different areas of your life and find balance to disperse your time and energy.

When we live in an imbalance, it causes madness, conflicts, and problems that lower the vibrations of our experience. We suffer in imbalance because we are running from one fire to put out to the next, never working ahead of, never being on top. The secret is to become aware of the deeper causes for the imbalances because once realized, they become the learning experiences and lessons that give us our wisdom. Creating a schedule is a terrific way to make the most of what you can do with the time and energy. This is done by understanding the areas of life, living connected with your why, and deciding how to responsibly disperse your time and energy for your optimal experience.

The areas of life are:
Work (purpose, passion, and prosperity)
Rest (replenishment, relaxing, and recovery)
Play (hobbies, adventure, and interests)
Relationships (friends, family, coworkers)
Life Essentials (taking care of the things that take care of you: house, finances, car, pets)
Personal Essentials (health, wellbeing, and hygiene)

Juggling these 6 areas can be exceedingly difficult when you are running on a mental program that does not currently support the dreams you have. Whatever you desire, and how your mind works to make use of your time and energy, must be synchronized together to put you on a path toward progressively realizing your dreams. How you intentionally spend, disperse, and allocate your time and energy is the key contributor to align your balance. Placing too much time and energy in one area can starve off another. Your moment-to-moment life, schedule and routine must be on the same page as your why, what matters to you, the relationships you have, and dreams you desire.

It is important to select the habits, thoughts, actions and what you need to prioritize to create your unique balance. With your plan in mind, fearlessly play around with what can work by referencing what helped others on a similar journey. Create an ideal daily, weekly or monthly schedule that is manageable for you to reverse engineer the outcome by beginning to dial yourself in and alter the plan when imbalances arise. This will allow you to live with a free and clear mind, knowing you are doing your best to live true to yourself and path. Balance is an inch by inch, step by step refining process. A balanced life will still come with its surprises, bumps, and struggles but by staying disciplined and consistent, you can improvise, adapt, and overcome all challenges.

Balance is not about achieving a destination, it is about remaining disciplined to what you must be responsible for, as things inevitably change you too must change with it, so that you are prepared for when opportunities present themselves to you. When levelling up, and taking on higher responsibilities, you will require different habits and thoughts for balance. Continued introspection and refinement is important to maintain as life is lived on many diverse levels, just remain in a constant state of growth toward your vision.

> Optimally disperse your time and energy
> toward balancing your responsibilities,
> relationships, and priorities.

THE POWER OF NEUTRALITY

Zero. The number zero is neither positive nor negative, yet can hold value as *digit* zero (10, 20, 30… etc.) and there is some wisdom in that. Excessive positive and negative perspectives can blind one from seeing *what is* in true reality. There are benefits to observing situations and circumstances from a *neutral* posture. Neutrality gives us clarity to see situations for only what they are and not what we *think* they are. A state beyond duality where you (the observer) are not separate from what is observed. No place for bias, no created or accepted construct to limit from your bank of references. It provides the ability to see without highly charged emotions swaying you or your truth away with a false sense of identity or a story.

To find this neutrality for yourself, use the tool below to help you begin to change the ways you think and see. This will grant you the ability to go inside and break through the barriers of the mind that have been placing limitations on your perception. Because "old you" would only focus on and think about seeing things from the view of the hard-wired and programmed past. To really free the mind, you must transcend beyond it, seeking a perspective beyond positive and negative, but a spiritually grounded one, an enlightened one, a neutral, loving, vibrant, and peaceful one. The true nature of what we are then mirrors the world from the inside out.

Picture a seesaw with +1 on one end and -1 on the other with 0 in the middle. Zero being the neutral center is the pivot and balancing point that is neither positive nor negative and not being emotionally swayed by the perspective of being emotionally up or down when looking at *what is*. It is at zero where you are in the goldilocks pocket of neutrality, a *just right* balance for observation. Now imagine there are ten increments of choice on both sides of the see-saw where you can shift your energy of emotions, thoughts, and behaviors, +1 being extremely positive and -1 being extremely negative. To remain in balance of neutrality, but still have our emotions pulling us in both directions of the see-saw, use your *intuition, the voice of truth* as your counterbalance weight for when you lean toward higher levels of positivity or negativity.

ACCEPTANCE BRINGS BLISS – THE THREE MAXIMS

The first step toward change is awareness.
The second step is acceptance. —Nathaniel Branden

By setting your intentions to place yourself in states of stillness and higher awareness, you begin to transcend the beliefs and lies coming from the voice of the programmed mind. Unlocking this step within yourself gives you the opportunity and courage to dive deep and confront your greatest mental, physical, and spiritual barriers, obstacles, limitations, fears, traumas, and stressors that block and estrange you from living with acceptance for self, for others, and for what is.

> **You must walk down the dark path of your mind to bring acceptance to *light*.**

This may mean you face what you fear and learn to stand like a warrior in observation, *accepting* what is and choosing to remain connected to your truth rather than the madness that comes with forms of non-acceptance. You now can begin the process of combing through every reason you have in your mind that you believe holds you back from the power of living in acceptance.

Ask: *Is this barrier, obstacle, limitation, fear, trauma, stress, or belief that denies my acceptance of self, others and what is, my own? Is this judgment, attachment, or resistance my believed truth?*

In truth, in present moment awareness, we unconditionally have acceptance for what is. It is our minds and environments that tell us the lies that have us hypnotized to believe in thoughts and forms of non-acceptance. We unnecessarily suffer when we live in non-acceptance because we exhaust ourselves by using our energy, time, and focus toward fighting against factors that we cannot control, adjust to, or eliminate, like swimming against the current of a stream.

> If you cannot control it, you must accept it.
>
> If you cannot adjust to it, you must accept it.
>
> If you cannot eliminate it, you must accept it.

It's not wise to waste your time, energy, and focus fighting *what is.*

It is wise to spend your time, energy, and focus *accepting* what is, because then you can shift your energy to what is within your own control; the way you *respond.*

In states of awareness, you will notice your mind's inner voice make a judgment about yourself others or a situation, it will try to pull you into forming an attachment for your sense of identity, or it will resist against something that cannot be stopped, and this is when your practice of acceptance awakens to make the inquiry once again; *Is this my truth?* Is this thought, this belief, this narrative speaking to me coming from the deepest essence of *my* truth in making this judgment, this attachment, this resistance?

If it is not in agreement with your truth, then why would you ever accept it? Ask yourself what and when this seed had to be planted for this lie, this false belief, this reason for non-acceptance to make its way to be in your mind, to be part of and shape your experience and perception? When you are in a state of stillness and follow down the rabbit hole of your mind long enough, you will see that every form of non-acceptance you hold is a believed lie that denies you the freedom to live through love unconditionally and in your truth.

> Unravel the lie, unravel the madness,
> and live in loving acceptance.

To find acceptance, start an open investigation in your mind. You begin with the obvious thoughts and forms of your non-acceptance that stand out to you. This is where you go through a personal realization that heals and lets go of the reason for the false belief of non-acceptance. Furthering in this process you will notice deeper and darker levels come to you. Many times, while meditating, exercising, or driving, I would have a not-so-random experience from my subconscious mind pop into my awareness that shows me the *root* reason for a dimension of my non-acceptance.

It is interesting because the mind that originally stored the memory is different from the mind that has the knowledge it has now. In this contrast you begin to see the moment differently, you see how everything is in service for your highest intention. It brought you *here*, so now it is the evidence to learn from and not something you ever had to suppress and suffer because of. The process toward acceptance is magical because you feel the emotional weight of madness lift off your shoulders. Like putting down some heavy luggage bags, there is a sense of relief the more you find within you and let go. Unraveling the layers of acceptance, you become lighter and *lighter*.

Each one of us has the power to search within our mind and discover acceptance hidden underneath the lies and false beliefs of madness that we have been taught. It is now *your journey* to cleanse, to discover what wounds must be healed, what beliefs no longer serve you, what psychological baggage must be confronted and released, which walls you built that need to come down, what darkness needs to come to light. Find all of what in your mind stands in the way of you unconditionally accepting yourself, accepting others, and accepting what is.

Eckhart Tolle outlined three "aspects of enlightened living" in his book A New Earth (Tolle, 2005). Putting these three maxims into daily practice will help guide the understanding of living in the bliss of acceptance;

1. It is wise to *practice* non-attachment.

Attachment is a dimension of madness in our mind because it creates and agrees with a false storyline of our culture and experiences, a false sense of identity that clings to the past and holds grudges, that places conditions on love, creates biased assumptions, expectations, outcomes for happiness, and excuses for why you are living in limitations. In thoughts and forms of attachment, we are truly a prisoner to our mind.

To practice non-attachment, you must use your awareness to filter and find what attachments are denying your truth. Start with something small like noticing when you produce an excuse for inaction. "I didn't want to go for a run today because it started to rain." Is the attachment to having perfect weather conditions the reason you run or not? Finding small attachments like this will show up to you increasingly, and it is important to scale the ego back from taking it personally.

You must be rational, open, and aware that these are the reasons that are holding you back from your high vibrational self. You must be committed to bringing yourself to a new level, one that makes the changes in your mind for acceptance. Eventually the small attachments you set your eyes to catch bring you closer to the bigger ones, the deep seeded, complex ones that are the imbedded causes of our suffering. Childhood traumas, trust issues, the pain from losing a loved one, there are attachments we hold and do not release that eat at our well-being in many ways. Finding the roots of our attachments and practicing love and acceptance until it is personally realized in your truth allows you to let go and break free from the continuation of its torment.

2. **It is wise to practice non-judgement.**
When we place judgment on ourselves, judgment on others, or judgment on situations and circumstances of what is, it's without foresight, without objectivity, without fact, it is merely a prejudice opinion, and this *belief* can be held in your mind without being filtered through your truth. Our judgments hurt us by narrowing the world as we see it. Closing off our

empathetic and compassionate listening and hearing abilities to only have eyes for the evidence that proves our false identity and the narrative from our false storyteller to be correct. All forms of judgment are made because of a believed reason for non-acceptance. We pin ourselves to seeing a world through the lens of "good" or "bad" when everything is *beyond* this duality.

> **As above, so below. As within, so without.**

"Why me" we cry out when something does not go our way. "What great luck!" We pridefully remark when things are *perceived* to work out. Imagine you are driving your car and you get a flat tire. Often, that flat tire would frustrate you while you make the judgment that this is a terrible thing that has happened to you, but what if it were the savior you could never see? What if that tire had not popped and 200 meters down the road in that future would have been a fatal accident for you? Would you be mad about that tire popping if you knew that it had just saved your life? What if the lottery you just won makes you happy but creates separation within your family and pins everyone against one another, becoming the catalyst of a complete family divorce, is your original judgment truthful? We must notice the many judgements we make and have them go through the light of your truth before they are accepted or spoken. Think and speak in acceptance and where there is no judgment.

3. It is wise to practice non-resistance.
Resistance persists and perpetuates within us by taking our highly charged emotions and giving away that valuable energy to fight what we disagree with through our forms of non-acceptance against what is. We may battle and fight with all our

might against what we choose to resist, but it is to no avail, it is rarely the energy that solves the underlying reasons or issues for the resistance. It is like choosing to talk about what you hate instead of placing that energy into promoting what you love.

Our resistance blinds us from acceptance by pointing our attention toward conflict and being against something or someone. We suffer what we resist because it always comes back to haunt when it persists. When we choose to fight or run away from our problems that does not necessarily mean that they go away.

To practice non-resistance, learn to do nothing. Simply observe yourself and the environment when resistance builds within the story of your mind and bring yourself to a place of empathy, compassion, and oneness. It may be difficult to break the cycle when resistance can highly charge your emotions but find a way for you to calm your mind and begin to set your eyes to see how acceptance can bring you closer to your truth.

In practice of non-attachment, non-judgement, and non-resistance, we unravel the lies that block the acceptance of ourselves, each other, and the world we share. In acceptance, we open our mind to connect to empathy, compassion, and our heart through *coherence;* the connection to the unconditional love that lives within us all.

HEART COHERENCE

Heart coherence is having our mind and heart connected in communication, cooperating with one another through our natural vibrations of love, compassion, and empathy in our state of being. Through practice and development of a deeper mindful connection and open communication to living through our hearts, we tap into our natural superpower of letting love be our voice that guides us through the moments of our life. Once we progress through our journey and grow our levels of awareness and acceptance, we heal and become *free* to experience more realizations and deeper connections with our heart in a way that ushers in unconditional compassion, empathy, and love to be synonymous with your truth and way of being. By establishing a personal connection to heart coherence, you no longer think or speak outside of your truth that creates excuses for holding back love for conditional reciprocations.

We start to live our lives leading by example with our presence of heart coherence. We help guide others to the words and vibrations of love, by communicating it and placing it on full display as it radiates out from every cell of our being. The more humanity begins to connect to heart coherence, the more will see it, feel it, and experience love in an unconditional way. Love is what truly has the power to conquer anything, so it is important for us on our individual path to understand and make this connection to our mind and hearts in a meaningful way. We must learn how to let love guide us and not illusions.

There are three ways to access heart coherence:

1. Practice intentional acts of self-love daily such as drawing yourself a bath or going for a walk in nature. Find habits that summon the power of positive feelings within you.

2. Meditation with the intention of communicating your mind with an open heart.

3. Noticing and replacing your conditional behaviors, habits, and patterns for love.

Doing these three things will allow you to begin growing your unconditional love to flow from you without ever needing a reason. It may be difficult to maintain this state for extended periods of time as your emotions, ego, and distractions will test how committed and truthful you are to being unconditional with love, because your mind's old ways will try and pull you back. This is when meditation will help guide you to feel the moments you are living in heart coherence and the moments conditional reasons have you lost this way.

You can analyze and see the moment you make a condition, and this is the belief that must be contemplated thoroughly, released, and let go. This begins a process of self-refinement, dusting yourself off and getting back on the horse until you find an unwavering way to master your mind, master your emotions and live in heart coherence regardless of what life throws your way. We epitomize and eternalize love by living through our own distinct connection to it.

As a man, heart coherence was not an easy connection for me to make. Before I had my breakthrough realization, I had only understood love in a logical, conditional, and limited way. It was through deep meditative healing of past wounds and current conditions, learning unconditional love through my close relationships, and practicing daily acts of self-love, that I was able to break through the barriers that were blocking my heart coherence.

Once you do make this connection (if you have not already), you will feel an incredible sensation radiating from your state of being. It is remarkable to compare the realization of unconditional love when all you have ever known is love in the conditional forms. That first glimmer of light breaking through changes the entire paradigm of your thinking process and perception, nothing as you once knew it is the same after. The more you guide yourself closer to connecting and thinking about heart coherence, the more you will speak and *feel* it.

POWER OF LANGUAGE 2.0

In recognizing madness, we discussed how the words and vocabulary we use can hurt us and dumb us down as a humanity. Words hold the power to paint our reality with ugly colors that have us experience, express, and communicate to ourselves and others in both toxic and beautiful ways. It is a choice within our own control to upgrade our communication skills, and this is a key element to mastering our mind by *reframing* the words of madness into one of radiance.

Reframing is a powerful way for us to change our words and language because it takes the conditional, the attached, the judgmental, the resistant words and phrases and replaces them with an empowering language of love. It can feel like you are learning to speak an entirely different language, but it ascends your energy and experience to a reality in the higher dimensions of being. As you begin to speak from love, it replaces the learned and programmed madness.

Let us try a few reframes.

"I'm so frustrated, I can't wait any longer!"

Reframes to:

"I must do what it takes to cultivate more patience."

"This makes me so angry; you never listen to me!"

Reframes to:

"I feel my opinion is not valued nor heard."

"I'm a picky eater."

Reframes to:

"I know what I like to eat."

There are so many dimensions of subconscious venom hidden in our words and language. Being mindful of the words you say truly matters because they plant seeds in our mind. It's wise to reflect on your use of language, walk like there are mirrors all around you, and *really* hear the words and phrases you internally and externally speak. Become aware of conditional, non-accepting words and language you currently use and open your mind to the truth of who you are by thinking and speaking that into existence.

FOUNDATIONAL QUESTIONS

To understand the foundation of where our minds are operating from, we must look at the questions that dominate our thinking mind.

Obviously, we have millions of thoughts and questions running through our mind daily, but it is at the core of our foundational questions that run and guide the program our mind is using. I would repetitively catch the inner voice of madness ask, "What do I have to do to get this over with?" Because this question was dominating my focus in most moments of my life, it caused me to be selfishly seeking shortcuts so that I could instead spend my time doing things that only served myself.

I realized that with my brain set with this question dominating my navigation of life like this was pulling *me* away from my true self. I was putting up a resistance towards accepting what is by trying to escape present moment reality rather than embracing it and immersing myself fully in it. Upon discovering these types of limitations that I had created for myself, I understood that I could consciously reprogram my mind with a new foundational question that was aligned with my true self.

I had to burn it into my focus, so each day I would meditate and surround my focus with an empowering question that would have me think in ways that would bring the truth of who I am into the present moment. I felt an immediate connection with "What can I add to this?" It became the center of my entire focus. I chose it to be my new dominant question because I knew it could serve me in ways that would help me find my truth. I needed a trigger, so whenever I would walk through the threshold of a new doorway and enter a room, whenever I caught my focus drifting off, or whenever I heard the voice of madness, I would stop everything I was doing and thinking about to internally ask, "What can I add to this?" Then I observe out in reality for a window of opportunity. This helped me enter a higher level of consciousness because no matter what the circumstances would be, I was able to bring all my true self to be fully present in the moment.

> **The first step is seeing, the second is *seizing*!**

Changing one of my foundational questions to "How can I add to this?" has impacted my life in ways that words cannot express. A real game changer for aligning me to my truth, my essence, my true self. I was more *me* in the moments of my life because I was starting to use this empowering question to queue my spirit to actively observe, participate, and create.

Questions are important because they are more abstract than fact. More open for discovery than closed off and logical. Questions pull your curiosity into the unknowns of your mind and connect you to search for what *you* think. If you were to use an open-ended question as one of your foundational questions such as "What am I going to do with the time I have, for the time I have it? Now something deeper will come, you will hear the truth within you that forces you to think freely compared to the reactionary and automated ways our mind runs.

I ask you to consider which dominant questions you currently have and reflect by asking yourself if these dominant questions of yours are going to lead you to your highest vibrancy making the largest impact. Are they pushing you to raise your standards for your life and overall vibrational frequency? Are they going to help you boost the dimensions of your reality? Do your foundational questions help bring you out of low vibrational states and back into your true vibrant self? If not, ask yourself what kind of questions you would need to use to prompt your truth to come out and be with you in your presence.

HEALING MENTAL TRAUMAS

One common denominator we all share in this human experience is that we all encounter forms of suffering in this life. We can be exposed to many things that traumatize our mind and spirit. No one is immune to this, and we experience and handle traumas in various perspectives. When we avoid grieving and healing from our struggles and suffering, we repress these traumatic events and memories (accidents, incidents, injuries, and tragedies) by building mental barriers that bury these unpleasant emotions and thoughts. Our past then dictates our present and future.

To unravel the madness from our mind, and transcend to the fifth dimension of being, we must muster the courage within ourselves to confront, heal, and release these repressed traumas that dwell in the deep recesses of our mind. It is not wise to allow any past trauma to hold you prisoner and deny the infinite potential of present and future realities.

Our *suppressions* of these traumas become our own self-inflicted *oppressions*, which lead us into *depression*. If we allow the struggles and challenges, we have in our life to continue to torment our present and future experience, we lose the true meaning of this gift of life. We are here to grow and learn from the past, not become paralyzed and tortured by it.

There are many stigmas in mainstream culture that teach us to cope with our traumas and this discourages us from building our spiritual and emotional intelligence. Living under archetypes such as learned helplessness removes us from our real power. Having an elevated level of emotional intelligence and control over your emotions is what will allow you to evolve.

We must find a way within us to let go and lighten the low vibrational emotional load we carry around. Guilt, shame, and fear deny our ability to live in truth; they weigh on our energy and being. You must come to an understanding with yourself that everything in this life happens **for** you. Everything had to be just as it was for things to be where they are now. You know that everything that happened cannot be changed, so it then must be accepted, and what knowledge you gained must become your strength and power.

I understand that it requires great personal strength and will-power to face and release traumatic events from haunting you, but when you do, the mental and spiritual slavery ends as we learn that true strength is found in letting go.

One of the biggest traumas we can face throughout living this life is "losing" a loved one to death. In one perspective of death, we can see that we lose something and someone incredibly important and close to our heart. In this view we continue reflecting over the pain and suffering of our loss, fighting against what we cannot undo, redo, or control. In another perspective, we can see life and death as synonymous, a changing of form. We realize that the only guarantee in this life is that death is inevitable to all of us. If we can find acceptance within our own sense of immortality and see in higher consciousness that we are eternal beings, we can empower ourselves through our grieving process to help us heal the wounds and events we face throughout our life.

When we grieve and enter the process of coming to terms with healing the ache inside our hearts after the initial shock to our reality, we can take a step back and see the bigger picture beyond our feelings of emptiness, numbness, and self-condemnation. If we are to find acceptance using a higher perspective, we can heal these deep traumas that inevitably happen throughout our life.

We must use a perspective that empowers us to carry on with the strength of our loved ones whether they are *here* physically or not.

Death shows us the powerful gift of life. At an early age, I lost **the** most important person in my life. My grandmother was the closest person to my heart, and we had developed such a deep loving connection to each other. We were twin spirits and inseparable. She developed a cancer that over months of time drained her energy and vibration to an unrecognizable and debilitating state. As I was young and slowly watching life be pulled away from her, my fear of losing her started to infect and impact my own life. She would always fight against the cancer that was depleting and exhausting her by using her powerful strength to communicate and engage with me whenever I would visit. I always cherished these moments, because I knew that it might be the last time I would speak with her. When she began to feel that the end was near for her, the things we talked about changed in an unusual way. It went from small talk and avoiding the reality of her inevitable death to the confrontation of it. She knew that her time was limited, and something must have hit her that our very intimately and private conversations were used as an opportunity to pass on the knowledge that would help me grieve her death and see the truth she discovered. She had to of been thinking about how much her death could traumatize me and she wanted to bridge me to seeing an empowering perspective so that I would not be tortured by her passing and future life traumas.

On one of my grandma's last days, I went to visit her, and she began teaching me how life is a celebration and that I should choose to celebrate her life at her funeral rather than be sad. She told me to speak to the people attending, share stories, memories, and highlights of her time and energy while on this earth. She promised me that she would always be with me in spirit, so that I never had to feel that we were separated by life and death. I remember having a sudden inkling in my young and developing mind that we are something more than our skin and bones. This incredible, strong, and beautiful woman could never die because within me, through me, her energy, her vibration, her spirit, would carry on. To this day I feel her presence with me.

> All things come to pass and life continues on.
> It is wise to understand that you are a part of it.

This event in my life was initially traumatizing because I did not want to lose my grandmother, but she taught me an especially important lesson to use for the rest of my life. In this tragedy, I was shown that when we suffer, it is a choice and a matter of perspective. My grandmother ensured to have the strength to live long enough and pass down to me her love and wisdom to not be traumatized by her death, or anything else, but instead to be illuminated by it. To never let any potentially traumatic event ever dim my own bright and vibrant spirit. She was an illuminator, and she knew I was one too. She was connected to the spirit within all of us and taught me that we are not here to be tortured and haunted by the events that transpire throughout our lives, but rather to be *strengthened* by them.

I realized that I had a choice to suffer in my circumstance of great loss or rise to the empowering state of carrying my spirit with the energy and memory of those closest to me regardless of if they were physically here or not. I began to understand the deeper perspectives of life when death hung in the balance. I transcended this potential trauma, and this life lesson helped me many times during my spiritual journey because I clung to my grandmother's love, wisdom, and strength as it showed me something that I feel so honored to share with you; It is wise to grant yourself the perspective and permission to not let the traumas you have experienced in your life to dim your bright vibrant and beautiful spirit from living anything other than your true self.

CHOICE – THE TWO WOLVES

Once you have reached a point in this knowledge seeking spiritual journey where you have noticed both the glimmers of light as well as the suffering we experience. Now that your perception is putting glitches in the matrix by seeing through the lies of illusion, you are left with the single most major decision of your life; the **choice** of which of the two wolves inside of you to feed.

The timeless story of two wolves comes from Native American teachings (Yeo, 2016), where a Cherokee grandfather is speaking to his grandson explaining his internal struggle. The grandfather explains how a fight is going on inside of him between two wolves. One wolf is anger, arrogance, greed, self-pity, ego, lies, inferiority, guilt, resentment, envy, sorrow, regret, false pride, and superiority.

The other wolf is joy, peace, love, hope, serenity, humility, kindness, benevolence, empathy, generosity, truth, compassion, and faith. The grandfather tells his grandson that this same battle is happening within him, and within every other person.

The curious grandson thinks for a second, then asks his grandfather "Which wolf will win?"

The grandfather replies: **"The one you feed."**

This gives one awareness and option of choice.

This story perfectly describes the ongoing never-ending spiritual journey as a process. The purpose of the journey is to find and know self and truth, to realize the nature of expressing your true essence as you live and share the experience of life with others. The process is the adaptable routine, the one that suits the true you, one that you can keep balance and harmony by using the knowledge you have gained from the journey and apply it to elevate your vibration to be your true self.

The point of this story is that we all have the balances of each of these wolves inside of us. We all hold the power of choice of which wolf we feed and which we starve through our thoughts and actions. No matter how far along your path, you will always carry the responsibility of choosing which wolf inside of you to feed. Now that you are arming yourself with knowledge, wisdom, and intelligence, you can begin to guide your choices by feeding the wolf with your hold on truth in present moment reality.

When you unravel the mind and think for yourself, you become powerful beyond measure. With choice you can feed the wolf that speaks your truth and elevates your vibration.

Our mind can be consumed with negative language and vibrations that cause us to think and speak in ways that create stress, tension, and dis-ease throughout our experience. In Unraveling the Madness from our mind, we have discussed the importance of establishing a daily meditation practice, and practical methods, tools, and processes that help us understand the *why's, what's,* and *how's* that unravel the madness from our mind. It's important throughout this spiritual journey to unlearn and unravel the madness programmed into your mind by replacing it with the truths you realize when connecting to yourself.

You must learn your own ways of absolving the tensions and diseases cast upon you by this illusionary reality. Each of us possesses the ability to rewire our mind so that it works as a beautiful servant to us, one that is connected to our true self, unconditional love and brings into existence the reality of our dreams.

We began this conversation by recognizing how illusion works so that now we can see what factors impact and affect our mind. This is important because once you can go beyond the lies you become aware of and learn how to think for yourself, relate to our unconditional love, and *live* by being your truth. You can now understand the grounding foundational effect of practicing daily meditation, the importance of mastering our mind, emotions, words, dominate questions, habits, behaviors, and priorities, the freedom of letting go by practicing acceptance, and establishing our mind and heart to communicate to one another and work in coherence. These are the essential tools for helping us reclaim our focus, our power, our freedom that gives us control over our own experience.

It is you that must take the journey within and unravel the layers that torment and entangle your mind. Once all the layers have been unraveled, the only thing left is the enlightening connection and realization of our truth/spirit/self. This connection causes a monumental shift in your perception that transcends your experience into the fifth dimension of being. The human mind is one of the most powerful tools in the universe. Everything that you see created first originated from the mind. For you to end your sentiments of suffering and guide yourself toward unlocking your greatest potential, higher purpose, and guided by love, you must unravel all the lies, false beliefs, habits, and behaviors that were programmed into your mind. Unraveling the mind will help you connect deeper to the mystical and divine aspect of self, your *spirit*.

CHAPTER FOUR:
UNRAVELING THE SPIRIT

You are a spiritual being having a human experience.

WITH YOUR BODY and mind unraveling and becoming more under your control, your experience of life becomes a blank canvas for the strength of your spirit to engage your world and reality with infinite possibilities. As we now dip into the mind and body being intertwined as spirit, we can unravel the remaining layers of madness and truly empower ourselves beyond the limitations of third dimensional reality.

When we sever the connection to our spirit, we lose our high vibrancy to the rat race, static and distortions that the third dimension of reality throws into our focus. This lures us into its machine that generates people who place profit over humanity, who suffer from self-loathing, lack of meaning and purpose for life. The system and its institutions specifically aim to drain and deflate us on a spiritual level, there is no question, masquerading this reality to confuse who and what we are by severing our connection to spirit. Knowledge about our spirituality is intentionally withheld and kept secret so that the common individual will become a thoughtless, powerless fool, easily swayed, controlled, and manipulated. Reconnecting with the power of our spirit is the greatest form of protest against the illusions of three-dimensional reality. Connecting with the spiritual dimensions empowers you by placing you in your highest and greatest vibrational state where you fearlessly rise above madness and suffering. In spiritual reconnection, you ascend and have the strength to live a life true to the very nature of who you are no matter the time or place.

Hundreds of years ago in Thailand, there was a village that had a giant golden statue of Buddha. When pillaging by foreign crusaders became rampant, there was a real threat to this village and most especially the golden statue of Buddha. The monks of the village wanted to protect this golden Buddha from being destroyed or stolen, so they devised a plan and took action to save it. They covered the statue in plaster and mud, pouring on layer after layer to hide its shine, beauty, and shape.

The plan had worked, but too well as the village was destroyed and abandoned while the golden Buddha became forgotten hidden under the layers of mud. One day, centuries later when the village was reoccupied, a little boy noticed a glimmering shine breaking through the layers of a mud pile. He began pulling the mud off and away and realized that under the mud there was a beautiful and magnificent golden Buddha statue (Tate, 2021). **You are the golden Buddha.** This spiritual journey will perpetually reveal to you the immense power of yourself under all the layers of madness and illusion. As you peel these layers off during this spiritual journey like the little boy from the story, the more of your true self you begin to reveal and recognize.

This chapter will explain how to remove the final fragments of madness that block our connection to our spiritual selves and how to unlock our *supernatural powers*. By understanding and connecting with our seven main chakras, the twelve laws of the Universe, the seven grandfathers, empathy, curiosity, imagination, creativity, the use of psychedelics, empowered by gratitude, and the power of perspective, we elevate our spiritual connection.

CHAKRAS — THE WHEELS OF HIGHER CONSCIOUSNESS

Chakras are the *wheels* of consciousness that exist within us as energy centers for self-alignment, knowledge, connection, and balance. They coordinate the reception, assimilation, and transmission of life energies. Becoming aware of each chakra that represents a different dimension of our overall consciousness helps our spiritual practice operate through *wholeness* and *totality*.

Balancing and harmonizing each chakra will open you to activating the latent power of *kundalini;* the coiled snake within each of us that is pure divine energy. This elevates your consciousness by unifying the polarity of powers within, of *Shakti* the goddess at the root chakra and *Shiva the god at the crown, creating a synergy of* masculine and feminine energies within us. The convergence of these energies transcends you to have total liberation from suffering and illusion. To activate this energy, practice deep meditation sessions and use Yoga postures connected with the respecting chakras. This *kundalini* energy lies dormant in every human, waiting for consciousness to awaken and *unleash.*

By awakening and aligning life force energy through each chakra up the chain along our spine, we receive our supreme spiritual power of access to source intelligence and collective consciousness. We enter the spiritual realm that communicates truth and knowledge to us in our present moment reality.

Through the chakras we become able to access higher intelligence, and self-knowledge.

> We are the cosmic antenna for which
> all universal energy and knowledge flows.

The specifics on the correlations of each chakra that I have used for my meditative journey were inspired by Patricia Mercier's work in *The Chakra Bible* (2007).

The Root chakra (*Muladhara*) is the first of the seven major chakras and is associated with the element of earth and the color red. It is located at the base of your spine and is correlated with trust and survival and is blocked by fear.

Meditation: Focus on the spot at the base of your spine and feel the stability of the earth element. Chant "LAM" to unleash the energy through this chakra.

The Sacral chakra (*Svadhisthana*) is the second of the seven major chakras and is associated with the element of water and the color orange. It is located just below your belly button and is correlated with creativity, sexuality, pleasure and is blocked by guilt.

Meditation: Focus on the spot a few inches above the root at your sacrum. Feel the fluidity of the water element. Chant "VAM" to unleash the energy through this chakra.

The Solar Plexus chakra (*Manipura*) is the third of the seven major chakras and is associated with the sun and the color yellow. It is located above the navel and below the diaphragm and is correlated with wisdom and will power and is blocked by shame.

Meditation: Focus on a spot behind the navel and connect with the vital energy of the fire element and yellow as the color of fire. Chant "RAM" to unleash the energy through this chakra.

The Heart chakra (*Anahata*) is the fourth of the seven major chakras and is associated with air and the color green. It is located at the center of your chest and is correlated with love and healing and is blocked by grief.

Meditation: Focus on a spot behind your sternum. Feel the expansiveness of air and the color green. Chant "YAM" to unleash the power of this chakra.

The Throat chakra (*Vishuddha*) is the fifth of the seven major chakras and is associated with ether, sound, and the color turquoise. It is located at the center of your throat and is correlated with truth and communication and is blocked by lies.

Meditation: Focus on the throat area, the color turquoise, and the limitlessness of space. Chant "HAM" to unleash the energy through this chakra.

The Third-eye chakra (*Ajna*) is the sixth of the seven major chakras and is associated with consciousness itself and the color blue. It is located between your eyes and is correlated with insight and awareness and is blocked by illusion.

Meditation: Focus on the spot between your eyebrows. You can even turn your eyes up slightly toward this point and place your tongue on the roof of your mouth. Chant "OM" to unleash the power of this chakra.

The Crown chakra (*Sahasrara*) is the seventh and final of the major chakras and is associated with cosmic consciousness and the color white and violet. It is located at the top of the head and is correlated with cosmic energy and spirituality and is blocked by ego attachment.

Meditation: Focus on a spot just above the crown of the head. You can also chant "OM" to connect your own consciousness with the universal consciousness.

These descriptions provide you with a basic understanding of the chakras. It is with your own internal meditative research that you must find connection to these seven main energy centers within yourself. Connecting with each of the chakras is relative to your personality and past experiences. For instance, as a self-described *earthy* guy, connecting to the root chakra was natural for me. Whereas I found difficulty in connecting to my heart chakra, because I was mostly shown conditional ways of love for most of my life. However, you may find that the chakras you find most difficult connecting with, can become your greatest connections once you envelop your focus and remove the blocks of its teachings. Once I removed the blockages that were keeping me from connecting to my heart chakra, I had a profound realization of the power of unconditional love, that only would have had such an effect for me because of the past being the way it was, a wise *teacher*.

The chakras bring us mystical and spiritual intelligence, but they also serve as a practical and pragmatic guideline to balance our overall health and wellbeing.

> Studying, connecting with, aligning, and *awakening* each chakra within you can provide significant realizations. These realizations profoundly change and challenge the paradigm of what you think and know about reality and existence.
>
> The truth cannot be told, it must be realized.

Carrying around and meditating with crystals connected to the chakras can help to elevate your presence with their conscious powers by raising awareness and building your self-knowledge. I have a shirt to represent each chakra and rotate through them once each week. My wardrobe rotation bringing awareness to each chakra really helps raise my daily awareness, connection, and focus toward balancing and harmonizing the chakra for the day. With this habit, my connection to each chakra expands and deepens each passing week.

Once all chakras are awakened and aligned within you, you transcend your present moment reality to be in higher dimensions of consciousness. This gives you an understanding of life that is beyond your previous level of comprehension. To truly know the depths of your spiritual self, you must be a forever student to the chakra energy wheels within you. Balancing and connecting to is a lifelong endeavor that you get better at with time. Once you become established in chakra meditation, you can go deeper into one of the most profound chakras, the third eye.

OPENING THE THIRD EYE

When your mind is clear and your third eye is open, you can see and know things that are taking place thousands of miles away from you. —Frederick Lenz

The Ajna chakra is known as the seat of the soul. The *third eye* is the spiritual gateway that opens our awareness to *seeing*. The power of seeing is beyond the psychological and physical perceptions, representations and memories that come from a programmed mind. It is associated with the pineal gland, which regulates our sleep and wake cycles and is sensitive to light. Let us break down its characteristics so we can get a deeper picture of its use in meditative practices.

The pineal gland is about the size of a grain of rice, shaped like a pinecone, and has little spiky hairs covering it. It's seated perfectly in the middle meeting point of our two brain hemispheres.

Externally, it's about an inch above the center of the eyebrows on the forehead. It has rod and cone photoreceptor cells just as our ocular eyes use to see, and because of that, there are many theories that suggest that in our evolution, our third eye was once on the outside just as Egyptian depictions of the eye of Horus on temple walls and on relics suggest. The pineal gland functions by producing secretions of melatonin, which is a serotonin-derived hormone that modulates our sleep patterns in both circadian and seasonal cycles.

In short, it sends signals for our awake and dream states. It receives information about the levels of darkness and light in our environment and doses our system the balance of chemicals accordingly. This regulates our balance of hormones to sustain self-homeostasis. The mystical powers of the pineal gland arrive when you learn the procedure of focusing your energy to force the secretions out on demand. Grab some popcorn because when you know how to open the third eye, the real show begins.

Pineal gland stimulation is a form of self-pleasure. It flushes out toxic energy leaving you to feel sweet and beautiful. It grants you access to the deeper dimensions of consciousness that transcend your meditative practice towards enlightenment through its connection with the Ajna chakra. Opening your third eye is one of the most essential elements of the spiritual journey to awaken and realize something that no words can fully describe, the elements of life, your truth, this sacred and divine power within you, the experience of oneness, and living in bliss.

Let us learn some techniques to pry open these potentially calcified, rusty gates that block our third eye.

First, it is imperative to establish a deep state of meditation. Once you feel in a state of stillness, shift your focus to visualize and connect with your pineal gland. Try and picture only this pinecone shaped figure resting in the middle of your brain. If possible, go out into nature and find yourself a pinecone to study the dimensions and burn the image into your brain for additional visual acuity. I prefer to see only the pinecone surrounded by complete darkness. Paying attention to the little hairs that cover it and watching as they dance and wave around as if it were floating under water.

To add depth to the focus, use your imagination to add vibrancy to the pineal gland such as giving it a florescent green glow. Place your focus again towards the details of where it is sitting in your brain and begin to focus your energy to only this spot. Use your breath to send your energy to it. Utilize the solfeggio frequencies of binaural beat frequencies to vibrate and massage this glowing, floating, pinecone, tickling and rubbing the hairs.

Imagine your focused energy to be something like the effects of the Ghostbusters Proton Pack that shoots out a string of vibrating light and blasts the pineal gland with all your life-force energy. To further enhance this experience, breathe in with your tongue touching the roof of your mouth. It is also helpful to imagine gently pulling your spinal fluid from the base of your spine, up and through each of your chakras, and towards where your spine meets the base of your head. Our breath works as the centrifugal force that illuminates our divine energy.

For this exercise, use exaggerated inhales like you're sucking soft serve ice cream through a straw as you draw up this fluid. Find any type of method that works for you to focus. You can visualize yourself as a boxer and the pineal gland is a speed bag getting hit repetitively or see yourself caressing the pineal gland in a loving way like petting your cat or dog. There are no right or wrong answers to whatever your imagination cooks up, just use the power of your visualization to focus on a form of stimulation.

The climax of this exercise will produce the secretion expelling from the pineal gland that is traditionally called amrita or nectar. It feels like a rush, a release, a *braingasm*. You will be able to feel the reward of your focused meditative effort as this secretion of natural brain chemicals coats your mind and lifts your entire being to a state of absolute *euphoria.*

The first time you open your third eye will be an experience you will never forget. Once you break through the threshold, gain experience with your meditation practice, and strengthen your focus, it will transport you deeper into seeing from the fifth dimension of being.

The moment I first connected with and opened my third eye felt like prying open a rusty, derelict steel shed door across my forehead, the type where the two sliding doors meet in the middle. I watched in third person as both my hands grabbed on the inside edge of each door. Tipping my head back, I began pulling them apart. In the background, I could feel something pulsing like there was an *unleashing* about to happen from behind the doors as if I were going to be letting something *out.* It was awkward and uncomfortable, because it felt granular and rigid as if sand or rust were in the door's sliding track.

I remember there was a screeching sound like nails on a chalkboard. Once I had pried these doors fully open, there was this vibrant purplish light that burst out to illuminate everything. There was a strange sensation like water dripping one drop at a time on my forehead, which was followed by a soft popping sound. A thick stem then burst through the middle of my forehead and blossomed into the formation of a lotus flower that was flourishing and settling with thousands of dancing petals. The flower was indigo in color, and I felt a deep connection to this lotus flower, as if it were an extension of my essence. No words came out of my mouth, just the sound "ahhhh."

This experience made me feel like a welcome mat was rolled out to a ceremonious ritual that would allow me to connect with the Universe. It was one of the most incredibly emotional moments of my life. I felt one within myself, and one with *all, simultaneously.* I thought this breakthrough meant it was all over at that point, but the interesting part is, as I look back now, it was just the beginning. It was a breakthrough to access a higher level of consciousness. There was much more inner work to be done, and I realized this was a tool I could use to go in and cleanse and heal my spirit.

That said, do not try to force any unnatural outcome. If you are not in a deep enough state of stillness and meditation, it will not happen. A distracted mind will not transcend. This can be frustrating, because you might really wish for it to happen, which can build a distracting pressure. The more you let go of trying to force an outcome and focus on the process of deeper levels of stillness, the easier it becomes. I have noticed that at first, this exercise would take me upwards of 30-45 minutes to achieve this blissful state of euphoria.

However, with time, patience, and consistency, I have grown my abilities and strengthened my connection of stillness and focus to be able to achieve this in just a few moments of mindfulness. My evidence is proof that you can possess this ability and use it at any and every moment so long as you continue to build your mindfulness muscles, so you have this supernatural ability in your back pocket.

It is important to consider the factors that place calcification over our pineal glands. It's vital to protect this gland so that it remains healthy for you to utilize in your spiritual practice. Avoid toxic chemicals, pesticides, herbicides and most importantly... fluoride! To decalcify the third eye, get restful sleep, drink plenty of filtered water, black coffee, turmeric, blueberries, walnuts, goji berries, cilantro, watermelon, bananas, honey, coconut oil products, ginger, chia seeds, hemp seeds, purple cabbage, sweet potatoes, dark chocolate, chlorophyll enriched superfoods, and lemon juice (Stokes, V. 2021). Yoga and other physical exercises, sun-gazing, and crystal use will also enhance the connection of the pineal gland outside of the meditative practices. Consuming these items in your diet, getting adequate sleep periods, and adding self-awareness physical exercises will help strengthen your connection to your third eye.

Once you open your third eye, the biggest glaring side effect to this change of view is the astounding flood of insightful observation you receive. It can be overwhelming at first. You will notice increased sensitivity to light and noise and the extremely heightened awareness of all that you see. You begin to see deeper with *spiritual eyes*. For instance, when you become in tune with this power and go to watch TV for the first time, you will know exactly what I mean. It is like wearing the glasses from the movie *They Live* (Carpenter, 1988), as you see all the underlying messages and bait being thrown at you to pull you back into the illusionary matrix of unconscious programming. You see and hear the beyond, and deeper than surface level.

THE TWELVE LAWS OF THE UNIVERSE – RULES OF THE GAME

Learning the twelve laws of the Universe and finding for yourself how to best apply them into your spiritual practice will help you master your reality, happiness, success, and prosperity (Singh 2021). These laws teach us that everything in this Universe comes down to energy, frequency, and vibration. They are the Universal rules of the cosmic game we are playing in our existence. Having awareness and knowledge of these laws allows us to see our world through spiritual eyes. These laws were discovered by humans throughout our history using observation and experience.

1. The Law of Divine Oneness — *Everything is connected. Every thought, action, and event are in some way connected to everything else. This is the law that others build off from. The*

Universe culminates its divine power in one singular energy from which all matter originates.

2. The Law of Vibration — *Everything is a form of vibrational energy. Energy is constant and cannot be created or destroyed, only converted from one form to another. As co-creators of this Universe, we can elevate our vibrations and consciousness to higher states of being.*

3. The Law of Correspondence — *As above, so below. As within, so without. This law emphasizes the distinct link between our inner and outer selves as one implies and compliments the other. Awareness of this law places you in higher consciousness as it helps in building communication of the higher and lower vibrations of the human structure.*

4. The Law of Attraction — *What you focus on grows. Aligning your personal vibration to what you desire to attract will result in its manifestation. When we think of negative vibrations, we attract more of it. The same is true with attracting a positive reality with positive thoughts. Use this law in your favor by being aware that you attract what you give focus to.*

5. The Law of Inspired Action — *Nothing happens in the Universe without taking some form of action, and when it is done under your own wholehearted intuitive guidance and truthful beliefs, you make quantum leaps of progress toward your desired goal. The power of using this law is harnessed by the convergence of your belief and ability to create in this Universe when taking personally influenced action. When we use inspired action behind what we do and create, things will seem to just fall into place as the Universe bends in our favor.*

6. The Law of Perpetual Transmutation of Energy — *Everything is in a state of evolution and fluctuation. This law governs that energy is never at a standstill, and that energy is in a constant state of motion. Tapping into this flow of energy will result in transforming one form of energy into anything you desire. Like an alchemist that transmutes lead into gold, this Universal law helps you transmute thoughts into things, the un-manifested into the manifested empowering you to create infinite possibilities from a higher consciousness.*

7. The Law of Cause and Effect — *For every cause, there is an effect. For every action, there is a reaction. All things in this Universe come from an origin whereby all thoughts and actions affect the entire Universe. This law is best understood by knowing that all things are connected and there is no separation from anything.*

8. The Law of Compensation — *Everything you reap is relative to what you sow. The Universe compensates for all our efforts and contributions. This means that all the rewards we receive are in exact proportion to the level of contribution we make. Our compensation is relative in that it may not come to us right away or in a manner we expect, however the reward will inevitably attract and manifest as your compensation.*

9. The Law of Relativity — *Everything is relative to the relationship and comparison to something else. This Universal law helps us broaden our perception as we only understand light because it is compared to dark, and we understand bad because we compare it too good. As we each undergo unique problems and lessons within our lives that strengthen and*

empower us, we can compare what we endure to what others have and this gifts us an expanded perception and perspective.

10. The Law of Polarity — *Everything has an opposite but are two inseparable parts of the same thing. You cannot have one without the other; there is no positive without the negative. For instance, if experiencing love is what you desire, but your deep subconscious mind is tuned to the energetic polarity of feeling alone, this may deny you the manifestation of your desire for love. To harness the Universal powers of polarity, you must tune your thoughts and energy to the polarity you wish to have your energy flow through.*

11. The Law of Rhythm — *Everything in the Universe works in cycles, rhythms, and patterns. Like a pendulum, the amount of force it requires to sway right is equal to the force to swing left. Everything is growing or dying, opening, or closing, rising, or falling, inhaling, or exhaling, there is always an oscillation, dance, rhythm, and flow. This law governs the surrender to what is instead of the resistance to it. When we use this law to go with the flow of things as they change, we oscillate into new beginnings. We strengthen our balance of thoughts and emotions when we understand the Universe works in rhythm.*

12. The Law of Gender — Everything in the Universe has *masculine and feminine energies. There is Yin and there is Yang, intertwined to make whole. Both masculine and feminine energies are present in each of us. Feminine energy is our giving and receptive side, being of primarily a compassionate nature. Masculine energy is our determined, action-oriented side, that holds the power of our will. Like our two brain hemispheres, left brain logic being masculine and right brain creative being feminine, these gender energies live within everything in the*

135

Universe, and it is wise to harmonize the utility of both genders to empower your experience of life.

Throughout my journey, I have personally experienced my own epiphanies and realizations that connected me to each one of these laws. At different progressions of my spiritual evolution these laws began to show me proof that there is a supernatural, spiritual element to life. I felt and experienced the unimaginable force of divine oneness once I had opened my third eye. When researching the science of cymatics (the physical manifestation of sound and vibration), I realized that everything we observe and perceive in physical and non-physical form in this Universe originates from a vibrational frequency. This deep and beyond way of using the laws of the Universe to perceive reality is revolutionary to the spiritual journey. With each understanding, personal connection, and realization of these laws, you can begin to harness their power and use these laws to shift things in your favor.

By focusing your energy on something you wish to attract, you will inevitably manifest it. When you realize your perception is relative, you can choose to expand it beyond your previous perception. When you see the cycles of math, nature, and life begin to correlate and converge you work under the knowledge of the Universal rhythms and cycles of life. When you discover both genders' energies within you and utilize this power to elevate your vibrations. When all these laws connect you begin to unlock the doors to higher levels of consciousness and your wisdom, knowledge and life begins to ascend toward a paradigm, perception, and reality of enlightenment. Each Universal law can and will have their own moment of shock and awe where a circumstance unique to yourself will cause you to *know* (not think) that this entire Universe is connected by the oneness between energy, frequency, and vibration.

Working with these laws helps us become a conscious creator of our own reality by understanding how we can align ourselves to the rules, frequencies, and Universal powers of each of these laws. It is believed that one who understands these laws to their fullest extent has the keys to all the mysteries of life. A master of the Universe.

THE SEVEN GRANDFATHERS – A SPIRITUAL MORAL COMPASS

The Seven Grandfathers are a set of teachings that demonstrate what it means to live a "good life." A spiritual barometer of morality that comes from Indigenous wisdom and knowledge. This wisdom is the *real history* that is passed on orally, but has been mostly beaten out of us, buried, and forgotten.

The seven grandfathers are the set of knowledge and guiding principles to be lived and empowered by. These teachings are passed on throughout the generations and used as the basis of guidance for their people. The seven grandfathers teach us an understanding of how as an individual as well as a community can be guided to live an enlightened and beautifully harmonious experience of life. A way of living with a solid foundation of spiritual values, morals, and principles that live *within* and *through you*.

The creator gave spirits known as the Seven Grandfathers the responsibility to watch over the Anishinaabe people. According to the Anishinaabe wisdom keepers, the grandfathers sent a messenger down to earth to communicate the values (Elder Eddy Benton-Banai, 1988).

1. Truth is represented by the turtle. To know all these things, speak the truth. Do not deceive others. The turtle was here during the creation of earth and carries the teachings of life on his back.

2. Humility is represented by the wolf. Know yourself as a sacred part of creation. You are equal to others, but you are not better. The wolf lives for his pack and the ultimate shame is to be an outcast.

3. Respect is represented by the buffalo. To honor all creation is to have respect. The buffalo gives every part of his being to sustain the human way of living. The buffalo respects the balance and needs of others.

4. Love is represented by the eagle. To know peace is to know love. Love must be unconditional. The eagle represents love because he has the strength to carry all the teachings.

5. Honesty is represented by the raven. Face situations with bravery. Always be honest with your words and actions. Be honest with yourself first, and you will be more easily able to be honest with others. The raven understands who it is and how to walk in life.

6. Bravery is represented by the bear. To face life with courage is bravery; a state of having a *fearless heart*. Do right even when the consequences are unpleasant. The mother bear has the courage and strength to face her fears and challenges while protecting her young.

7. Wisdom is represented by the beaver. To cherish knowledge is to know wisdom. The beaver uses his natural gift by altering the environment for his family's survival.

These seven grandfathers offer us spiritual guidance to live a human life. They harmonize man and nature and offer a set of principles that give our morality wisdom and knowledge to steer life in the right directions.

I connect daily to each grandfather in my morning meditation by spending a moment reflecting and providing myself with evidence of times in my life when I *embodied* the strength of each grandfather. I carry each grandfather with me in my perception wearing them like a badge of prevalence. Each of the grandfathers combine to bring a dimension that gives strength to my spirit as I navigate through my day and life.

EMPATHY — THE POWER OF UNITY

Empathy is one of the most important connections to make in the spiritual unraveling process. Empathy is integral to the foundation of seeing the world in a united, connected, and loving manner. It is true unconditional love and respect for divine oneness intertwined. As madness works to separate and divide us from self and each other, empathy is the universal connector.

Empathy can be described as:
- Seeing through the eyes of another,
- Compassionately and actively listening to another,
- Placing your heart in another,
- *Walking in someone else's shoes.*

Equality for humanity balances on the depth of empathy that you, me, and we as a collective tribe of people have for one another. You must feel deeper than surface level judgements and assumptions to understand a person and their perspective. We do this by bridging the connection to our own heart coherence and learning how to connect it presently to be in another. It may take a lot of effort and focus to strengthen your empathy muscles because you have not received much information, or seen many examples of how to use it, but just as with any other muscle, you can build upon it through practice and grow your capacity for empathy. The more time and energy you give to practicing empathy and the clearer you see past the veil of illusion, the more you see how connected we are, and the complexities of life become remarkably simple.

Madness takes us away from ourselves and forces us to think and act in ego and lies. Learning how to increase our empathy breathes love, compassion, and understanding into our own world and the one around you where we can transcend the illusions that filter and dilute our language and actions of unconditional love.

We have two ears and one mouth for a reason, and that is because we should listen twice as much as we speak. To practice empathy, you must use your focus, your heart, and active ears. If you listen with your heart to the words people say without judgments, assumptions, or clouded references, you will be there in the moment, locked into the world and reality of another to just see it compassionately from their view. The more you include this into your daily presence, the more you will feel the pulse of the universe operating your life on higher vibrations.

Misunderstandings become understood, and we all deserve the right to feel understood. Wisdom is knowing that we all suffer from the illusions of madness and that we are all from one of the same collective humanity. Empathy helps us align to the fact that we are a people of One. With empathy in our presence, we can enlighten the world to its frequency by highlighting it through our thoughts and actions.

GRATITUDE

Gratitude is a remarkably powerful positive state of being that helps unlock our spirit to experience life in the deeper elements of love and appreciation. It helps unshackle us from perceiving and experiencing toxic thoughts and emotions by shifting our focus to find and search for new things each day to appreciate and be grateful for deeply and meaningfully. Gratitude puts you in the spirit of giving and aligns your energetic frequency with abundance and the law of attraction. Gratitude is finding appreciation for the small things, like the air you breathe, and monumental things, like the life you live. It is appreciation for the mystical and the sacred in life.

In practicing gratitude daily, your entire world will open once you program its frequency into your present moment way of being. This has your vibrational energy download and emit its frequency making everything and anything feel entirely possible. When we use this energy and operate our lives from the foundational basis of love and appreciation rather than envy, frustration, resentment, and regret, we transcend beyond illusions.

There are many ways to practice gratitude daily to help place your state of being into a vibration of appreciation. You can start with a gratitude journal and write down three things at the start of each day that you are profoundly grateful for. You can choose to thank someone each day for a small act of kindness or express your feelings to someone you care about. You must have a deep personal connection to the meaning of what you are grateful for. Simply saying the words without holding a deep value behind them will not connect you to truly experiencing the power of gratitude. Be sure to give this practice the focus it requires to place yourself in this empowering state of being. Gratitude within yourself promotes gratitude throughout, so the more you practice and focus on it in your daily presence of spirit, the more you will experience and receive it. When your energy and vibrational frequency operate on the level of gratitude, the entire Universe bends for you, and the world is at your fingertips.

I recall the exact moment that I broke through the barrier for the first time to not just speak and desire gratitude, but profoundly experience it in the truest sense. It provided me with a reference and something that I could always come back to and reconnect with in my spiritual journey. My state of being was so electrified because I could finally understand the empowerment and why so many people were preaching the attitude of gratitude. I would recall this moment and place myself in the feeling repeatedly.

It happened when I had just returned home from my second overseas deployment with the Canadian Armed Forces. I had been away from my home and family for six months where I was wishing every night for just a moment to be on the other side of the world and spend some time at home again. It was the second week of January, so it was extremely cold that day and I was still in the cultural shock of not being permanently surrounded by thousands of constantly chattering people. The moment happened as I began walking down my hallway toward my living room that opened into a triangle shaped log cabin. I remember thinking to myself "Is this a dream? Am I experiencing this right now?" but kept walking slowly forward. Gazing at all the subtle details of my beautiful home, I remember feeling this warm sensation coat my entire body and feeling as if everything I had endured was leading to this moment. I then sat down on the two oversized steps that went down into my living room. I had a vinyl record on playing Prince's Purple Rain, and straight ahead of my view, there was the fire in the fireplace I had just got going. My spouse came out of the kitchen behind me and sat next to me handing me a hot tea. This was the moment that everything changed as it created an intense sense of complete and utter gratitude. I was in awe of how beautiful life is and can be. The strange thing was, this was nothing too out of the normal environment of what I have lived in and experienced thousands of times before. It was because of the months of separation from everything I loved and cherished, the comparison of being away for so long, to be there and have this moment, the one I had wished for and longed for every single night I was away, for this moment to be real and as my current reality, it *hit* me. I really basked in the moment that was unfolding in front of me. It was the deepest sense of gratitude I had ever experienced in my life. This moment gave me something I could never forget; life is and always has been lovely, sacred, and divine. We often let so many things be in the way of our happiness, but when you scale your perception to understand that it is truly a privilege to be alive in the now, you understand the power of gratitude.

CURIOSITY, CREATIVITY & IMAGINATION

A curious and inquisitive spirit is one filled with energy that thirsts for more. Curiosity is the magic in life we taper off from and lose as we age and grow up. As we become adults, we condition our sense of self and truth to the comforts of the known. Our curiosity is what pulls us into the growth of the unknowns, where we have the wherewithal to expand our creativity and explore our imagination and learn new things. When we do not spend much time growing our knowledge in new and spiritually expansive ways, we lose that spark to explore our imagination, creativity, and curiosity. We do not *see* nor *seize* the opportunities of the present moment. When we exercise our imagination and creative muscles, we find ourselves solving our own problems, opening our mind to new things, different angles, deeper perspectives and having less prejudice.

If you begin to see deeper, then you can think deeper and work outside the box to solve your own problems rather than relying on others to do so. When you make a habit of learning more about what your curiosity has brought to your attention, the question then becomes: *How deep down the rabbit hole do you want to go?* Does your curiosity pulling you places not give you alarm bells about what you need to do? When we are guided by our curiosities, creativity, and imagination, we are in a powerful state of being that transcends our fears, doubts, and insecurities.

To fully embrace the art of our creative, curious, and imaginative spirit, we must have *belief* and *faith* in ourselves. We often outsource our beliefs to ideas, celebrities, sports teams, or religions, but to really raise your spiritual practice, you must believe in yourself and the immense power you have as a unique co-creator of reality. In doing so, you will access the powers of your evolving true potential.

If we use old references for a new world, we stay in the past as the present and future slips out of our control. You must bring yourself back to being child-like, inquisitive, imaginative, and creative without the attachments, assumptions, or judgements we have been programmed with. To do this, look out at the world and observe it through the eyes of your inner child or with *naked eyes,* because if you have the curiosity to dive deeper into what things truly are and mean, you will gift yourself a deeper understanding about yourself and the power of how much you do not know.

FINANCIAL LITERACY

I wish to offer you a few lessons to think about that helped me in my spiritual journey and process to get out of the quicksand of debt and running on the treadmill as a clockwork dog living paycheck to paycheck. We all deserve an abundant and affluent life, and it starts with building knowledge to begin to *see* and *understand* the rules of the game that we are all in but have not been introduced to. Having financial freedom welcomes and reveals our spiritual freedom.

There is too much focus on the ends (having a boatload of money, being financially free) and not enough focus on the means, the ways in which we can create several streams of income.

Research has shown that the average millionaire has *seven* streams of income. Most people rely on one, their job. When I first heard about the seven streams of income, my next thought was, "How could I possibly create and set up multiple streams of income for myself outside of my job?" It was this open-ended question that sparked a journey to expand my understanding of the *game* of money. Setting up these multiple streams took time. I had to study and learn how to invest, how to create passive incomes like real estate and authoring a book. I kept hearing people telling me they did not know how to do the things I was doing, and the truth was neither did I at one point, but I was not going to let that stop me from dedicating time to learning. You must have patience, delay gratification, and invest your time, energy, and attention wisely.

Whether raised in rags or riches, it is of zero relevance to your potential future reality, because your financial reality in life is entirely reliant upon **how** you *think, see, feel, and do.*

For instance:

"I don't *think* I can," versus "I think anything is possible."

How have you set up your brain to think?

"I *don't* see myself making it anyways," versus "I *see* this as an opportunity for growth."

How have you set your eyes to see the opportunities that exist in each moment?

This helps you seize opportunities because your vision has an open focus.

"I don't *feel* like doing the work," versus "I *feel* as if all my desires have been already satisfied."

How you feel plays a major factor toward your state of being. To be attracted to energy and money, the way you feel must be aligned with your clear and defined financial goals.

This helps you live in coherence. A highly vibrational energy and perspective helps us claim understanding over our emotions from fear and negativity. Money does not operate on a frequency of negativity; it is a vibrational mismatch.

As most money issues originate from our inability to handle our emotions, it makes you wonder, *why aren't we formally taught tools for emotional intelligence?*

"I can't *do* anything about it," versus "I can *do* just about anything."

How limitless is your ability and capacity to do it?

Do you have the discipline to show up and do the work, especially in those moments or days when you do not feel like it?

These reframes help you see opportunities, think creatively, act and build momentum. Money is attracted to those that have set themselves to be attractive to it.

Ask yourself and answer this:

How could I think, see, feel, do and be more attractive to multiple streams of money?

You must dig the well before you drink the water.

Most people are waiting with their hands out asking for water instead of picking up the shovel to dig the well. You must wish for things and be intentional no doubt, but if you are not living in alignment and disciplined toward actioning the habits of what you are asking for it may never manifest, because you cannot expect the Universe to do the work for you. For any stream of personal or financial success, you need the discipline to act without getting emotionally tripped up with impatience or by having irrational expectations.

1. *Decide* how it is going to be for you, what it is going to take.
2. Be *intentional* about how you wish to fill each precious moment of the day.

3. *Discipline* yourself to show up for your actions to success no matter if you *feel* like it or not. (You will never regret doing the work that is necessary.)

4. Have *patience* for the nature of things to develop.

5. *Commit* your energy toward seeing things through. Do not stop believing.

6. Write out your clear, prioritized plan to achieve your financial goals.

7. Focus on doing one thing at a time to the best of your abilities.

8. Wake up with a ritual that aligns you to this.

This is how you learn your way to dig the well.

Once the well has been dug, imagine now, a manual water pump has been installed. If you do the work and pump from the well, you reap the rewards of filling up a glass of water. Some will do the challenging work of gradually building flow and momentum, then settle and walk away once their glass is full of water (instant gratification). You allow the momentum of centrifugal force from the work you have done to settle back down, leaving yourself to start over from the bottom and work hard yet again the next time you are thirsty.

This is like slaving yourself to a job just to pay the bills.

Whereas if one were to delay the instant gratification of settling for just a full cup of water and continue the momentum of pumping, the water builds the force to flow in a stream that requires little physical effort thereafter to fill *countless* glasses. This is the secret. Learn how to dig, learn how to delay instant gratification, see the bigger picture to utilize your arduous work and *systemize* streams of income passively, and actively to fit your desired financial goals. Otherwise, you will be another human being used like a battery by the elite players in this game of money.

Imagine if it were true that soon you were going to receive a hefty sum of money. As an exercise, accept this as a truth within yourself right now. Once you feel that freedom, you might notice your shoulders relax, but your head might be going Mach 1 processing all the avenues that open from the money. Pay off a debt, upgrade the car, buy a new house, et cetera. If this were true in your reality, you might start living differently, acting differently, and feeling differently. The illusion that money carries convince most of us that it is the primary *condition* required for us to feel at ease within ourselves. It is as if, *only* once you have a certain self-designated amount of money in our bank account, can we grant ourselves the permission of freedom in experiencing pleasantness within and pleasantness throughout. This internal electricity of freedom existed within you all along, you've just attached a conditional monetary number value that your mind and ego would like to see before it allows you and that beautiful energy to radiate and transcend your state of being.

This is the *doublethink* that often gets in the way of attracting money. Our vibrations must be aligned to allow the attraction. It is important to visualize and be in moments of gratitude to increase this attraction. Having your thoughts focus on abundance attracts abundance.

Ever hear about those lottery winners that quickly find themselves back in financial issues once again? Or celebrities, athletes and musicians that are filing for bankruptcy? Being rich or poor is not a fact nor is it a destination, it is entirely a *psychological state of being.* If you do not understand or set your mind to generating, seeing, creating, or attracting money, it will always slip through your hands.

> When we acquire liabilities, our money dies.
> It runs out.
> When we acquire assets, our money grows.
> It keeps flowing.

If we took all the money from the rich and gave it to the poor... eventually, with enough time, the money would fall back into the hands of the rich, and the wealth gap would re-establish itself. How is this so? Because the rich understand that having emotional intelligence pays, having patience pays, knowing how to think, see, and use leverage. They know how to see opportunities when others see problems. The rich have and use knowledge of how to generate it, create it out of thin air, attract and manifest it into their lives, because it is a part of the processing of how they think, feel, and are. Poor thinking is easy, it knows how to spend, wallow in circumstance, and create excuses.

Using my own example, I recall who "I" was that put me in piles of debt using the wrong means to declare my sense of self-significance. I would buy wonderful things to surround my life with while using borrowed money, all in an act to appear well off to others. I saw the world from such a superficial, material, and limited point of view. The truth was though, that because my focus was so wrapped up in running on a treadmill with my financial problems, and continuing to chase after things that would in the end only create more financial problems down the road, I was blind to living my life with the unconditional joy, and freedom of feeling what you think money can bring when you have it in abundance.

The hack is: you must act and be present in your life, as if every ask you have, every desire has *already* been satisfied. You must accept and feel this as truth deep in every cell of your body. Have your entire being clearly visualize downloading the feeling of the financial situation you desire. Practice this visualization daily. This is where the illusion of money has blinded us from experiencing that true sense of freedom it provides. You will notice that over time your thoughts and actions will begin to be aligned to this frequency that attracts money. This realization becomes reality as you learn to live this as truth and embrace it. Find it within your own personal vibration and match the frequency of attracting abundance into your life. Like tuning into a radio station, dial into feeling the vibration of attraction and abundance as if it were part of every cell, every strand of DNA. Once you have it, resonate this energy out of your spirit like striking a gong or tuning fork. Carry this energy around with you always and allow external reality to merge with your internal.

For the vast majority, we are brought up in an environment where openly discussing finances is considered rude or *taboo*. We can be scolded at an early age for bringing it up or in adult social circles because of the embarrassment and fear that it carries for some people.

Poor (thinking) people avoid talking about money in an abundant sense because it is not a reality they subscribe to. Where most people feel like they do not have the abilities, mindset, nor tools to get their financial situation under control for themselves, they accept within themselves and almost surrender to their existing (perceived) reality keeping them stuck in the same financial situation.

It is a shame that it is not normal or "accepted" to learn money management skills or openly discuss healthy money habits (most especially to our watching and listening children and youth). We have been programmed mentally to include so much of our sense of self-worth to coincide with our current financial situation because of a made-up pressure. Subconsciously, we broadcast poor language when we say things like "that's expensive" or "I could never afford that."

If you think you can, you can. If you think you can't, you're right. —Henry Ford

---

Increase your value, increase your wealth. At any school you will find a janitor whose job is to keep the place clean, and you will find a teacher whose job is to educate the students. Both go to work in the same building, and both are paid a wage as compensation for the value they bring. The **value** they bring to their positions is the difference in the financial compensation they receive. Both are human and of equal opportunity, both are using their time and energy to earn their wage, yet one position is seen as more *valuable* than the other and that is because one is *perceived* as more *replaceable* than the other.

So here is the daring question: How could you begin to increase your value while reducing your level of replaceability?

What is possible that you could do today and the next day to sow the seeds for future prosperity?

In the poor mindset, there is no thinking about the reality of a bright, prosperous, and undoubtedly, inevitably successful future. The poor mindset keeps people on a mental treadmill licking their wounds, wallowing in their situation and circumstances. However, planting seeds of prosperity is exactly what you must do to shake out these poor thoughts. Do the things that grow your finances mentally, physically, and spiritually. Find the things that elevate your vibrations and light you up. Take on small disciplines such as a personal exercise program, these will transition to the bigger disciplines that bring you attraction and manifestations. Be excited about your future and what you can make possible with the right mindset.

- Give more than you take.
- Delay gratification.
- Curb your expectations.
- Master your mind and emotions.
- Stay the course.

Applying these principles will help increase your value and therefore your compensation.

The day you sow the seed is not always the day you reap the harvest. If you get discouraged and are impatient, your expectations will distract the focus of **execution**. This may lower your personal vibration to a point where you are not sowing the seeds of prosperity.

Falling in a rut sucks, and it is hard to pull out of, but with just one act, one thought, one workout, one morning meditation, you can shake it off to get you right back on the horse and carry on. The problem is, if you do not sow seeds of prosperity, weeds will grow automatically.

Money can get you out of a problem. But it does not fix the psychological program. It is like a band-aid for a gunshot wound. If your thoughts are poor, you will become your own self-fulfilled prophecy, in that you get what you ask for.

In our "educational" years while in school there is no mention of financial literacy or proper ways to manage money. Skills like how to read a balance sheet or even just understanding the difference between assets and liabilities. These skills are foreign to most and it is the very reason people develop a habit of being boxed and limited into thinking and living poor.

Those that have this poor mindset have it deeply ingrained and programmed within their core sense of identity. If you are bent on comparison, competition, and conflict with others, you are taxing your mind with useless stress and wasting your *valuable* time. You can work hard, but if you do not compound that with working smart simultaneously, you will be the rat running on the spinning wheel, going nowhere sabotaging and limiting your *infinite* potential.

Are you the type that looks under all the rocks?

Opportunities are present in every moment. Are you looking? Are you *paying* attention?

They call it *paying* attention because it *pays* in future dividends what you give your attention to.

Think of your focus like an investment.

Beyond hard work, you must become the visionary, the thinker, the see-er, the connector, the problem solver, the person who recognizes patterns for potential, notices a demand, creates the supply, crafts the sketches, gathers the permits, goes the full length to see it through. You must become the one who "fixes the toilets" by doing what everyone else *will not*. They may say it is "too much work" or "I don't know how to do that" and never do anything to figure it out, keeping themselves full of excuses and thereby avoiding the progress of learning, growing, and getting things done!

It is *that* level of human you can reach within yourself when you grab life by the horns, by disciplining yourself to becoming accountable to the best version of who you really are deep down. Take what you have around and use it to create the moves that plant the seeds, that ripple the waves that set you free, financially, and spiritually. You must live knowing the reasons for why you do what you do.

Half Full? or Half Empty?

Annoyance? or Opportunity?

Problem? or Solution?

Life is what you *think* it is...

The way you see things has an exponentially dramatic effect as you move in life from moment to moment and from interaction to interaction. Awakening to this opens you to see the interconnectedness that we share amongst each other, and that very notion is the catalyst that welcomes that Law of Abundance we were discussing (there is ample money for anyone who *knows* how to acquire it and keep it flowing). Building that pipeline to let everything you dream come naturally to you.

Start creating opportunities to be of contribution to someone, anyone, or a large group of people where you share the lessons of what got you through. Step up outside your comfort zone at work, lead a connection with others over similar interests and pleasures or just simply...solve other people's problems that you *teach* and *discipline* yourself to enjoy solving. Then you will never "work" a day in your life.

In spirituality, you see the oneness, the human view, the real satisfaction, and personal growth that comes with charity and contribution. In contribution, you find yourself as the healer, the doer, the fixer, the hero of your story and inspiration for everyone else watching your moves. All on purpose to be and to live the life that makes you most fulfilled, satisfied, and therefore spiritually and monetarily abundant.

We are all capable of creating wealth, abundance, and a beautiful life for ourselves as well as for those around us when we just *decide* for real, to be deeply connected and disciplined to dedicate our lives to patiently living through alignment with our true self and heart. You must learn for yourself how to match the vibration of attraction and abundance of money.

SPIRITUAL SEXUALITY

In elevating our levels of consciousness along this spiritual journey, we become less compulsive with our thoughts and actions, and more open with our perception. Through this expansion, we can observe dimensions of our life to recognize and clear blockages to harness the true power of our divinity. Our connection to sexuality is one of those taboo dimensions. Old perceptions that see sex as a sin or merely a physical act can deny our access to our sexualities power.

Though our old references, social stereotypes, and pornography, we might see the act of sex to extract pleasure out from someone else, and in this, we misdirect the potency and purity of our natural sexual energy. We can develop addictions and dependencies with our repressed sexual impulses that have us chase an illusion of pleasure and happiness. If we give mind to a story that causes issues of sexual inadequacy, we can push ourselves to forms of avoidance that compartmentalize and create blockages. The blockages we develop within our sense of sexuality are simply a misperception and misidentification of something that is beyond these labels. When we approach our sexuality by sharing our connections and feelings of love, the fundamentals of our life and perspective dramatically change. Our sexuality is then experienced as a sacred act of divinity.

> **Sex is the union of two becoming one.**

What we are not taught or told is that our sexual energy can be used as an instrument to raise our level of consciousness. Many ancient cultures and traditions were aware of the vibrant force of kundalini's energy within us and its link to sexual energy. By creating polarity between the masculine and feminine energies within us, through this union, we generate a magnetism. A bioelectricity that dissolves illusions and ego and awakens the forces of love within us. This magnetism elevates our experience tapping into higher levels of consciousness.

Through karmamudra and tantra, we transform ordinary pleasure into vehicles for spiritual transformation and liberation (Richardson 2003; Ferrara 2015). By practicing tantric sex, we can weave the physical and spiritual elements of love within us. This practice focuses and emphasizes the importance of *intimacy* during a sexual experience. Tantric sex is less about the orgasms and more about the *intercourse.*

Understand that there is a potent force within all of us in our natural sexual energy. Once unblocked, harnessed, and channeled, we can alchemize this energy to bring more connections of love into the dimensions of our life. Through a deeper connection to our sexuality, we can openly express our vulnerabilities of love and build healthy relationships.

It's wise to reflect on our own sexuality when in the process of raising our levels of consciousness in this spiritual journey. In my own inner searching I found blockages within my sexuality that stemmed from a past sexual partner. Each time we would embrace each other intimately, to no fault of her own, our moments of intimacy became so painful for her that it created a tendency within me to be worried about her wellbeing. Beyond the pain, my partner was also extremely paranoid of getting pregnant, so she would make me show her the condom and put pressure on the sperm each time to prove there was no leak or break. This made me feel uncomfortable and eventually I would create excuses not to be intimate with her just to avoid the situation. This tendency to avoid sex spilled over to other partners. It was not until I self-reflected that I realized this root cause that was preventing me from freely exploring and expressing my own sexuality. It was uncomfortable for me at first to face my sexuality, but in being open and introspective it helped me cleanse and unblock the illusions that keep me from higher levels of consciousness.

GETTING THE LEAD OUT – SPIRITUAL CATHARSIS

You may have a lot of past program patterns coming back to you as you try and step out of a shell that you are not. When journeying this new path, it is important to set aside time for the release of your suppressed, depressed, and repressed emotions. You may need a spiritual cleanse, a *catharsis*. *Getting the lead out* is a great tool to exercise your demons by allowing all the powerful pent-up energy buried deep within to come to the surface and be released.

Releasing this energy from within is very therapeutic and sooth-ing for the spirit.

It is important to plan beforehand, because this energy is pow-erful, and it is important to ensure that no one will be harmed by what you are about to do. It is not wise to allow your pain to become someone else's. We often take our catharsis out on people and things by harming them and doing what does not serve you on this new path. It is time to direct this energy in ways that do serve you and evolve to serve beyond yourself. When this power-ful energy is within your control, you can empower yourself to rise and be a better version of yourself. Harnessing this energy can help you move mountains.

If your suppressions are emotional, journaling is a fantastic way to get the lead out because of the therapeutic effect you receive when getting your thoughts out of your head and onto paper. If you feel as if no one listens to you, well, at least *you* will. As the words begin to hit the page and are directly pulled from the suppressed feelings that were buried within, you feel the amazing effect of clarity of your problems as you release them by *letting go*. You will feel light, and ready to move forward, carrying on with your life without the weight of your thoughts weighing your present and future down. This empowers you to see clearly and without your demons changing who you are in the present moment.

If your suppressions require a physical release, you can tap into channeling this power by releasing it through your exercise workouts, a jog, a hike, or a Yoga session. You can throw rocks as hard as you can in the woods, a ball at a wall or just scream out everything you got deep down in there.

Getting the lead out is the spirit's therapeutic release that helps us spiral out from the walls we have put in the way of our bliss-ful self. Most are scared to acknowledge the fact that these feel-ings inside exist and need to be released. They deny it, say they are "fine" and let the pressure continue to build until they do or say that thing they did not mean and act out of true self. Humble yourself to the fact that we humans are sometimes overrun with what life throws at us, and what I mean by that is … it is okay to not be okay. However, it is wise to do something about it. Learn to leverage this energy by alchemizing and transcending your suffering by channeling it to become your power.

> Catharsis purifies our spirit.
>
> It frees us from the expensive pain of suffering our suppressions.

PSYCHEDELICS – ABRUPTLY REMOVING THE FILTERS OF THE MIND

On this journey, you may develop curiosities about the use of psychedelics to connect you deeper with the spiritual realm, help dissolve the ego, heal traumas, or transcend other forms of suffering you may experience. Psilocybin, LSD, MDMA, and DMT are psychedelics that offer different experiences that can lead to profoundly deep realizations by removing the filters of the mind as you enter higher dimensions of consciousness that may challenge your beliefs, profoundly change your perception, mood, and cognitive processing. With psychedelics, you can experience philosophical and existential insights that have you think, see, and be in higher states of consciousness.

In this lifting of the veil, a new paradigm and dimension of reality opens where all your previous knowledge, understanding, beliefs, and perspective are radically *challenged* as what you feel, and experience unquestionably expands you beyond the limitations of the programmed mind. Psychedelics have the power to connect you to directly to experiencing *pure love, bliss,* and *oneness with all things.* You perceive self, other people, situations, and life in a way that your cognitive capacity may have never experienced before. It brings you to the core of who and what you and the universe really are by deconstructing and disintegrating the entire default mode of your mind and ego operate on.

A "trip" will expand your perception and current belief systems by showing you the "other side" of life as you instantaneously take quantum leaps of perceptual understanding the Universe. You may notice heightened sensations, time may become distorted, hallucinations of geometric patterns, and a sense of euphoria. Your perspective during a trip expands so greatly that life afterwards is radically different as you cannot pretend that you did not see what you saw or feel what you felt.

Once the effects of a trip do wear off, you are left with the breakthrough reference of the beyond; that *other side* you experience provides you with evidence of the real possibilities of transcending to realms and dimensions of higher consciousness. The aim is then to learn how to merge your everyday natural cognitive state of being closer to this blissful and euphoric psychedelic state.

Lacking respect while recreationally using psychedelics misappropriates the sacredness and potent healing power that these therapeutic medicines possess. Psychedelics offer a beautiful and meaningful expanded state of consciousness that transcends the self beyond the mind where you can unravel the false self and false identity.

A psychedelic experience offers you a chance to take a step back from everything you think and know to fundamentally understand the inner workings of your own mind's psychology. You see that there is so much more than what you know about life, and that your previous perception in comparison seems so narrow and ignorant. Using psychedelics is beautiful and can provide a life changing moment, because once you realize for yourself that we know so little and that there is something much more spiritual to this experience of life. Gifting you the chance to enter the doors and windows of opportunity in your own mind that fear and limitations would normally inhibit.

> **You step through the shadow.**

These psychedelic experiences offer *teachings* that are unique to you and can surface root traumas and memories that have been suppressed and hidden for decades within your conscious and subconscious mind. These unaware and unexpressed suppressions within can be released when under the influence of psychedelics because you have the courage to face everything you fear. This is the most pertinent and incredibly powerful benefit of using psychedelics. You become free to truly sit with and heal a lot of things that have been holding you back from living a beautiful life as you come out from the experience able to live without their false limitations from ruling over you. The full scope of the experience of psychedelics cannot adequately be explained with words, however the personal insights you receive from the experience can bring upon extraordinary and monumental positive shifts into your life.

I know for certain that I would not be where I am mentally, physically, or spiritually without the use of psychedelics and most importantly psilocybin mushrooms. From the first time I consumed this sacred plant medicine, I was marveled by the effects of abruptly stepping into a higher state of consciousness. After the initial nausea subsided, the high vibrational effects began to set in and work their magic. (I recommend starting with a 1.5-gram dose and eventually working your way up to a 3-gram dose once comfortable with doing so). As the effects pull you beyond your mental programs and illusions, you will instantly feel what I describe as pure blissful unconditional and universal love that reverberates throughout both mind and body as a life enhancing spiritual experience. You will feel a bright energetic glow resonate from you. It is such a unique experience that it is like nothing you could have ever felt before. As I feel this pure love, I have the sense that I, you, and everything else is a part of the same living breathing source of creation. In this state of love, all I desire to do is give it out in abundance by sending it out through my energy without ever worrying about giving away too much, because I have a deep sense of knowing that there so much to go around and the more, I give the more I receive, and it is positively infectious.

During my first psilocybin trip, I recall instantly feeling like I was intensely teleported to a state of being that allowed me to freely love and let go of everything keeping me from happiness. I could forgive every reason I had for held guilt, for every intolerance, judgement, assumption, and expectation that was denying me from living under the truth of this blissful feeling of unconditional love I was experiencing during this trip. I was forgiving of everyone who I had perceived to have "wronged" me throughout my life. I was seeing and feeling my entire life happening a million miles a minute as I was sitting still and tranquil meditating in my living room. After the initial rush of love flowed through me, my dormant sense of creativity, imagination, and curiosity was sparked and awakened. I had serious interest and thirst for higher knowledge and understanding of things just like I had when I was a child. The things I would always put off or limit by saying "I don't know" now became what I was most interested in and inquired about. A lot of what psychedelics do is connect you back with your inner child, the purity of who and what you are before the world gave you reasons to live in suffering.

Throughout my trips of psilocybin, I healed the deepest wounds of my spirit that were denying my true happiness and joy in life. Every single time I would take a trip, some deep and dark memory from my past would come to surface and it was so incredible to me, because I had the ability to see the memory from a different, older, wiser perspective and recognize that letting it go and sending it off was what I needed to do to avoid harming my way of experiencing life, or natural state of being. To this day I still consume this sacred plant medicine because of the connection I've built to it through all that it is done for me. It still helps me find wounds that heal my past as I continue to transcend to higher and higher levels of consciousness. Magical mushrooms have a big place in my heart for what they have helped me through on my journey. The confidence and courage they provided me with gave me strength and solace to elevate my consciousness.

I must admit that when it comes to MDMA, I personally do not have much recent experience with its spiritually healing properties. However, there have been many studies showing remarkable results for the treatment of post-traumatic stress disorder (Mitchell. 2021). I had used MDMA quite frequently during my late teens to feel euphoric in what I remember as the most hostile and depressing years of my life. I would take MDMA at least once each weekend for about a year to put myself in a fantastic and incredibly positive mood that felt much better than the depression and anxiety that I was often experiencing. The problem I faced was it was illegal, and I did not want to do anything so wrong that I would end up in trouble. I had an inner civil war about this medicine that on one side of the coin made me feel euphoria and the other side was the consequence of it ruining the trajectory of my life. My fear of "getting caught" stopped me from continuing to enjoy its beautiful effects. I had taken MDMA with such an immature mind and perspective at the time. I am open to reintroducing myself to it considering everything I have been through spiritually. I think it would be remarkably interesting to experience MDMA without the fear, paranoia, and guilt clouding over me.

Albert Hoffman was the Swiss chemist who had first synthesized, ingested, and learned about the psychedelic effects of

lysergic acid diethylamide or better known as LSD when researching medicinal plants for the pharmaceutical laboratory he worked
for. When he isolated and synthesized the fungus *ergot* from the
drimia maritima plant (which makes sense why it has such a
similarity to the effects of psilocybin), he accidentally absorbed a
small trace amount through his fingertips and quickly discovered
the powerful psychedelic effects. His by-chance trip took him on a
journey that revealed a message that he then dedicated the rest of
his career, time, and energy on this earth sharing with the world.
Albert Hoffman said when asked about LSD, "It gave me an inner
joy, an open mindedness, a gratefulness, open eyes, and internal
sensitivity for the miracles of creation...I think that in human
evolution it has never been as necessary to have this substance
LSD. It is just a tool to turn us into what we are supposed to be."
He explained his personal trip as "affected by a remarkable rest-
lessness, combined with a slight dizziness. At home I laid down
and sank into a not unpleasant intoxicated-like condition, char-
acterized by an extremely stimulated imagination. In a dreamlike
state, with eyes closed, I perceived an uninterrupted stream of
fantastic pictures, extraordinary shapes with intense kaleidoscopic
play of colors." (Hoffman, 1960). This description best describes
the experience of LSD.

LSD was a very bright and enlightening and hallucinogenic
experience. I had some incredibly insightful visions on LSD. It felt
like I could sense beyond our normal abilities. I could see what was
not there but was. The experiences I have had with LSD were so
incredibly fascinating and mind bending to float through the infinite
potential of the universe freely, creatively, and lovingly. LSD marvels
at you by expanding your mind so vastly beyond anything you have
experienced before that it gives you a reference of the infinite for
when the effects wear off. You are launched into a world of visions
that connect you to higher thoughts that help you understand your
life relative to the universe in a spiritually expansive way.

Dimethyltryptamine or DMT is something much different than every other psychedelic. A trip of DMT offers the user an experience that shifts your very being beyond the physical plane. After consuming DMT, you will enter a paradigm of reality filled with *remarkable* geometric shapes, colors, and things that you have never experienced before and are hard to explain in words. The initial shock and awe of what you sense striking you with colorful, beautiful spectacles shifts to a meeting of an *entity* or sometimes a group of *entities* that present themselves to you in an extremely friendly manner. In my experience, there is always a feeling that whoever or whatever these entities are is *familiar*. Familiar like the unconditional love you feel from your mother, and at the same time the great relationship you have with your best friend. These entities act as a guide, like an angel, that is there to help show me something important. If you get overly marveled in the mystical experience, it is hard to focus on what the entities are trying to show you. They demonstrate something to you as an alien form of communication, and on some weird level, you can understand them and respond by going back and forth with communication that is beyond words. I have received cheerful signals from these entities whenever I would guess the right answer to whatever they were trying to sequentially show and tell me. It is like a game show studio audience responding with applause or a bell ringing that you did the right thing and won the prize. The entities would seem so cheerful when I would guess the right thing of what they were trying to communicate to me, I could tell it appeased them. I only use DMT whenever I feel the need for some guidance, because every time I take a trip, I am shown a *particularly* important demonstration or symbol that instantly reveals to me the exact lesson I need *most* in my life at that time.

I believe that a DMT trip is the closest thing to the dimension or realm we enter when we die a physical death. It's so perplexing to me how familiar it seems even after taking my first trip.

The trip only lasts about five to ten minutes, but it can sometimes feel like an hour has gone by. I recommend every human on this earth to experience DMT at least once, because if we all did, we could all live with the knowing of the highest form of technology on the planet. If we all experienced a DMT trip and knew that we all had experienced it, we could explore better questions about the mysteries of our existence rather than wasting so much energy creating wars over our differences.

In taking psychedelics, be sure to consider the **set** and **setting**. The set, meaning the mindset you have going into the experience, must be clear and intentional, with a goal in mind, with what you expect to learn, understand, or resolve from the experience. I always create a ceremonial ritual when consuming psychedelics to honor and respect the sacredness of them. The setting, meaning your environment, must be comfortable and familiar, one that will not distract you from your desired experience. Utilize music, aromas, and lighting to create an atmosphere that allows you to relax and invigorate your heightened consciousness.

All the knowledge from this book can immediately be understood in a single psychedelic experience. Dr. Timothy Leary said, "I learned more about psychology, about the human mind, about the human situation in five hours after eating these mushrooms than I had learned studying, doing research in psychology, and treating people as a psychotherapist." (Leary 1996). When he was being interviewed and said this, the man interviewing him was staring at him with such disbelief in what he was hearing. The psychedelic experience really does offer you a beautiful way to experience the beyond, by raising your level of consciousness up in frequency to experience it.

While regular doses of psychedelics provide a fantastic opportunity to experience an expansion of consciousness and healing, *micro-dosing* offers everyday benefits without the hallucinogenic and deeply mystical effects. When taking a small micro dose, you will notice all your senses sharpen, your focus will be dialed in, your cognitive functioning, mood, and pain tolerance will elevate and increase.

It invigorates and inspires your creativity and imagination by allowing you to effortlessly place yourself into empowering flow states. It is something that I personally use because it boosts my spiritual connection, energy, desire, productivity, coordination, and courage to face my fears. The greatest benefit is that it keeps you present in the moment connected to infinite possibilities. You feel super-you, like in the movie Limitless or like Super Mario who ironically also took mushrooms to power up.

There must come a time when we accept and realize that these sacred and therapeutic plant medicine psychedelics are nature's tools to heal and empower the human spirit. The fact that anything naturally occurring is criminalized makes you wonder. Especially when there is overwhelming evidence that they were widely used in many ancient civilizations and indigenous cultures for the purposes of connecting closer to God.

Psilocybin, MDMA, LSD, and DMT offer different experiences to heal the mind, body, and spirit. It is important to do your own research and consult your doctor or psychologist, if necessary, before taking any of these sacred plant medicines.

DEVELOPING A POWERFUL PERSPECTIVE

The fixed mindset tells us that our personal qualities and attributes such as intelligence, skills, and talents are limited in that they cannot be changed, evolved, nor be improved upon. It tells a story based on the past, one of lack and disconnection from truth, and one that success is only available to those who are naturally gifted. We must learn to tap into the ability to silence this voice that stops us before we even start by empowering our attitude and perspective to see through the lens of the constant growth our true unlimited potential has.

When we fix and limit ourselves with a narrow perspective, we lose sight of the boundless opportunities for growth that our real self and spirit desires and dreams of. The mediocre and mundane life we fall into, resent, and suffer by is lacking the higher perspective of what could be. Sometimes we need to climb to new heights to see a broader view of things. We do this by raising our awareness to adopt the growth mindset.

The growth mindset helps uncage the personal beliefs we have deep down to realize that by effort and hard work, any skill and ability (within the parameters of physics, biology, etc.) can be grown to a level of *mastery* on a long enough timeline. Everything becomes possible when utilizing greater perspective to seek out the connections, information, inputs, and strategies that elevate our ways of thinking and seeing. The growth mindset can inch you closer to a goal that satisfies your spirit in ways that instant gratification and praise could never do.

To grow, we must be gritty. Being gritty means to keep moving forward no matter what. It means to fight with all you have in your spirit for millimeters of progress and growth. To be gritty means you can fall seven times yet get up eight. With grittiness apart of our perspective, we hold the keys to our self-ascension that begins to open the doors to higher consciousness and success.

THE FOUR P'S OF A POWER PERSPECTIVE

Persistence — Persistence is the drive to remain focused on the task at hand. Having the discipline to show up even when you do not feel like it. Too often we fail because we lack the persistence to keep driving ourselves to accomplish what we set out to do. We get lost in the drama and story of how things should unfold and wish for the perfect conditions to accomplish the things we deeply desire to do. Placing persistence into your perspective will help you rise to the inevitable challenges that present themselves on your journey. In persistence we are dedicated to the hard work necessary to accomplish remarkable things. Persistence means not waiting for it to get easy but remaining loyal to the path you have chosen by any means necessary.

Perseverance — Perseverance is different from persistence in that in perseverance we are pushing through the barriers of failures. In perseverance we are beyond the struggle with the motivation to keep doing what we are doing, and instead we are actively applying the teachings we learn from our iterations of effort and most importantly from the failures we endure as valuable lessons. In perseverance we rise to the true test and strength of our will. While we can persist in running on a treadmill, we still get nowhere. Perseverance takes persistence to another level in that it infuses knowledge and intelligence into our perspective. Persistence is valuable as it serves as the precursor for perseverance, it takes your perspective to channel your effort from the benefits of working hard to the intelligence of working smart.

Patience — Patience is an asset to our perspective because it gives us the higher understanding and knowledge that on a long enough timeline, anything is possible. When we add" yet" to the end of your sentences, it shifts our perspective in a powerful way because we begin to anticipate that things should always be under our control. Our expectations, prejudice, and assumptions deny us the patience for allowing things to naturally unfold. Without patience in our perspective, we urge ourselves to rush the process and get so focused on the pot of gold that we forget to enjoy the rainbow.

Placement — It is wise to place yourself in multiple perceptions and timelines using different lenses, wearing different hats of observation to transcend the illusions and lies of madness truly and fully. Too often we do not put into perspective the centuries of our evolution, the history and wisdom of our ancestors, or are confused by the immaturity of our mind throughout the distinct phases of life such as when we transition from teen to adult and become responsible for ourselves. It is wise to place your perspective in an attitude of gratitude and seeking our own constant evolutionary growth. There are benefits to you as an individual as well as others that you connect with once you journey through this process of spending the time to unplug, find yourself in the darkness and build upon your perspective through the knowledge and understanding you receive about yourself, our humanity, it's needs and life in general.

In persistence, perseverance, patience, and placement we shift our perspective to higher levels of consciousness and being by seeing wider, deeper, and from angels that act like angels that guide us by showing us a fuller truer view of circumstances and situations. In this higher perspective we can mitigate living in regrets or have lack of perspective denying us the sustenance of a better overall experience of life.

THE WARRIOR SPIRIT

We are all warriors in spiritual warfare. Because life is not always going to be easy, and because there are dark energetic forces that try to break our human spirit, it is important to tap into our powerful warrior spirit within each of us. Our warrior spirit is there to guide us through our many battles. For battles with self, battles with negativity, and battles with illusions, we must learn to harness our spiritual strength.

There is something within each of us that knows we cannot remain quiet or stand idly by when our beliefs and freedoms are on the line and being taken away. We must cultivate and nurture our inner warrior's strength to not give ourselves away and die from a spiritually deflating system and reality. We must not break to the will of spiritual oppressors. We must learn to find the fight that exists within us.

When I first joined the military to be a Canadian infantry soldier, I was put through the process of being emotionally, mentally, and physically broken down to my most fundamental levels. I was away from family and friends, deprived of food and sleep, had zero free time and under the heaviest amounts of stress and pressure I had ever endured. I was broken, and when all my walls came down, I could be *rebuilt. From civilian to warrior.* This process taught me that I had a *spirit* within me that was beyond the identity and story of who and what I thought I was. It taught me that I could always quit, so why would I quit now? I had experienced the evidence for myself that I could do the impossible when connecting and embodying the spirit of who and what I truly am.

A warrior lives his life by a set of ethics:

A warrior lives his life by design, not by default.

A warrior lives his life by choice, not by chance.

A warrior makes changes, not excuses.

A warrior improvises, adapts, and overcomes in all situations.

A warrior lives in the belief and faith of their own capabilities.

A warrior endures all challenges.

These factors help us understand what it means to be *resilient.* I had realized that if the army could break me down and build me up to be a warrior, I had the power to do something similar to make me a better human being. I could take my spirit *from lost and aimless to found and purposeful.*

A warrior is a worker for the light. A fighter and protector for the spirit within each of us. We all have a message of importance and the ability to make a difference. You may be beginning to sense that you are here to be a part of the change of our history, as a chosen one. One who understands the war in our minds, the war in our hearts, the war in our streets and communities. Chosen to live beyond yourself as a beacon of light for higher dimensions of consciousness by showing that there are *other* ways to live, navigate, and experience this meaningful gift of life. One without the need for unnecessary suffering.

UNRAVELING THE SPIRIT WRAP UP

With self-knowledge and understanding of our seven main wheels of consciousness, the twelve Universal laws that operate as the rules of the game we are in, and the spiritual moral compass of the teachings of the seven grandfathers, somewhere in the connections of all three, we unravel the spiritual dimensions of our consciousness. Tapping into our spiritual super consciousness that helps us reconnect with our empowering states of being empathy, curiosity, imagination, creativity, third eye, sexuality, and gratitude. These help to align us to the energetic vibrational frequency to live our life in the truth of our spirit.

Psychedelics serve as a connector for us to achieve the higher dimensions of consciousness. Removing filters from the mind such as limitation and fear, we transcend the programmed mind to observe our mind's psychology from a higher perspective. We can heal the spirit of who we are through these plant medicines if we respect and honor their healing powers.

Spiritual catharsis *channels* our energy to work for us and beyond us and does not allow it to be used against us. And finally, the growth and gritty mindset supercharges our fighting spirit for our perspective to live aligned to who we are.

PART THREE
TRANSCENDING TO THE FIFTH DIMENSION OF BEING

THE FIFTH DIMENSIONAL state of being is the reality of freedom, bliss, love, and oneness.

You experience life in truth, as self, with unconditional love and one with all things.

The end of unnecessary suffering is the metamorphosis toward enlightenment.

Experiencing life in the fifth dimension is your personal heaven on earth. You are:

- Connected with present moment reality.
- Ceaselessly evolving and expanding into your higher self and purpose filled work.
- In love with the process of levelling up dimensions of your life and experience.
- Experiencing *intensity* for living fully and *ease* from unnecessary tensions.
- Sensitive to experiencing all things in the Universe working in energy, frequency, and vibrations.
- Your choices and decisions, thoughts and actions are connected to self, love, and truth.

May these words help navigate you out of the cycles of suffering you experience and transcend your consciousness to the higher dimensions of being where you realize and greet the power of being your true self.

CHAPTER FIVE:
THE END OF SUFFERING

HOW DO WE end the suffering we experience in life? How do we reclaim our power, freedom, and liberation? It is not so simple, but the answer is through rebirth. A transcendence of consciousness that permanently takes hold of your present moment reality. Beyond suffering, we are free to live deeply connected and aligned with our mind, body, and spirit. Free to live true, fearless, pure, honest, and loving.

Once we begin the process of spiraling out from an identity and story of who we are not, and have our first deeply realized *epiphany*, the paradigm of our perspective fundamentally changes in a radical and profound way. We then begin to operate our lives from a wider perspective and our spiritual eyes have us experience increased a-ha moments, epiphanies, and realizations that connect and correlate. As your view of yourself, life, and reality vastly broadens, a bigger picture begins to become clear.

At some point, you get pushed to the *edge*. Your journey takes you along to see and collect information and all your connections and epiphanies form your new base of knowledge. This provides you with an overreaching intelligence that something must *break*, there must be *something more* to all this. So instead of dipping your toes in, you jump. The moment of surrender is the ultimate clairvoyant epiphany. The one *instant* that enlightenment hits you forever breaking you through the barriers and blockages to experience the fifth dimension of being. This can be the most life altering occurrence one can have.

We shift the journey into the process when we transcend suffering. We know what we must hold on to because we know what it can be. And once you know the other side, there is no going back. We suffer only until we realize it is unnecessary. We rise to our power. We learn to fight for what we believe in with courage and live by our own morality and personal integrity. We master time and guide ourselves by our intuition. We learn to protect our self and energy with an impenetrable force field and access higher knowledge by quantum entangling our consciousness to source intelligence.

Unraveling the final layers of madness, we peel it all off and away, forever shedding the skin of being the victim, and the one who suffers. Going through a *metamorphosis* from human doing to human *being*.

> **We are *something more* than the skin and bones, suffering, constructs, and illusions.**
>
> **When we end our suffering, it is the moment we transcend.**

TRANSCENDING FEAR AND LIMITATIONS

Fear is a powerful inhibitor to our higher self and consciousness. It freezes and paralyzes us or gives us reasons to run and flee. To end suffering from our fears, we must learn to have the courage to stand in our power. Our fears only come to us from ignorance in our perspective. From death, to spiders, or speaking in front of a large crowd, what we are seeing, judging, expecting, interpreting, or assuming is false evidence appearing real. When we learn the power of championing our fears and transcending them, we begin to take our power back and become unstoppable. You become supercharged when you stand in your power to face fear because you shift your perspective to see through the beliefs of your spirit.

In the moments of human decision making, you have three responses; **Flight** where you run and flee, **Freeze** where you are paralyzed from taking action or a making a conscious decision, and **Fight,** the power of what you have within, the human spirit, your will.

You are left with two choices: Forget Everything And **Run** or Face Everything and **Rise.**

You always have the option to fight and if you really want to end the pain and suffering you experience in your life, *you must be all in and willing to fight for it* by facing everything and rising. Those who flee and freeze will cycle through the continuation of their suffering.

When fear shows up in your experience, use it as a key indicator for an opportunity to stand in your conscious power. Use it as the route you should take, and not the one you should avoid. When you decide to face the uncomfortable with your courage, you will begin to give yourself the evidence that fear is only an illusion of our perception.

> Our fears can either paralyze us from taking courageous and bold actions in our life or they can guide us in the direction of our highest self.

As I had a deep desire to take this path of self-seeking to end the suffering I was experiencing, I had many of my own fears try to block, stop, and force me to submit and quit what I was doing.

For every new level there is a new set of fears that you must fight to transcend and find a way through. Our greatest fears carry with them the greatest opportunities for our growth and evolution. How we choose to face our fears brings out the best of us, as what scares us and challenges us helps change us. What should really put fear into our mind is being trapped in the cycles of suffering that deny us a beautiful life.

From fears of being judged for having the struggles I had, to fears of not finding answers. What I had come to realize was that every time I had a fear present itself to me, I would muster the courage to push myself through and this gave me a newfound strength within myself. I noticed that whenever I would step into whatever fear I had, it would empower me in a way that I had never felt before. I began to collect self-evidence that challenged the beliefs that were causing my suffering. My fears transcended the beliefs I had of who I was and what I was capable of. The most extreme form of self-empowerment. I dare you to face your fears, because if you do, you will be illuminated by realizing how much of a perceptual illusion our fears truly are.

Up until 1954 running a four-minute mile was believed to be an *impossible* feat for human biology. This was an accepted limiting belief amongst medical professionals as they warned anyone daring to attempt the four-minute mile that it was potentially *life threatening* because it could cause the heart to *explode*. This created a fear and limitation for a lot of people from even thinking about attempting to run a four-minute mile. Sir Rodger Bannister was not one of those people and achieved the impossible. On May 6th, 1954, Sir Rodger Bannister ran a mile in 3 minutes and 59.4 seconds and shocked the world (Runyon, J. 2014).

This accomplishment gave the entire world the breakthrough evidence that we can transcend the fears and limiting beliefs of others. Just 46 days later, John Landry ran the four-minute mile. Since then, **thousands** of people have accomplished this "impossible" endeavor as well. The lesson from this story is that if we accept the fears and limiting beliefs of others, we can suffer living a life caged by limitations and one untrue to ourselves.

Sometimes we just need our own permission and vision to believe anything is possible. When we do this, we tap into the power of bringing ourselves to the very edge of our own potential. We each can be a pioneer of proving what is possible when our beliefs are transcended beyond the fears and limitations of others. When you transcend the fears that place limitations on your beliefs, you step closer to living in what truth you discover within yourself.

SHEDDING SUFFERING THROUGH QLA

When you notice yourself being a prisoner to your own mind or if force fed someone else's tainted view of reality, you would have a choice to do something to exit the cycles of suffering. Now that you are steering the wheel of your experience, you can empower yourself with a daily exercise that helps dissolve the programs and patterns of the false self, story, and illusions with three simple steps:

Step 1: Quiet
Whatever is pulling you, use your present moment consciousness to quiet it immediately. In stillness we can think and be clear. Establish tranquility as your primary foundational basis for your decision making. First quiet the noise in your head and tune out your judgments of the environment. *It is wise to quiet everything and operate your decisions from clarity.*

Step 2: Listen
Listen for messages beyond words and language. Listen to the subtle energies of yourself and your environment and the relationship

between the two. Listen to what your inner self is saying. Listen to what your truth is saying. Listen to what your intuition is saying. Listen to what your environment is saying. Listen to what you can learn from or add to your present moment reality.

If nobody is *really* listening, then nobody will feel heard or understood. We are programmed to wait for our turn to talk. *It is wise to be a great active listener.*

Step 3: Accept
You must remind yourself to accept *what is*. After a personal epiphany of acceptance, you hold deep meaning and value to the truth of it. You understand that we only suffer in forms of non-acceptance. To end the suffering, and to seed your mind with a new program of acceptance, we must bring it into our daily practice until it transmutes into your present moment reality. *It is wise to have acceptance for what is.*

Through these three steps in your daily spiritual practice, you can remove the final layers of suffering from your experience. By quieting the noise and using a clear foundation to make our decisions, we can open our ears to actively listen to ourselves, others, and the environment for a proper read on present moment reality. We then funnel this information through our acceptance, we think, act, and be our most true self in the present moment.

The more often you practice Q.L.A. in your daily life, the more suffering you will shed. Be who you are in your life, rather than the consequence of everything that has happened to you.

HUMILITY — I AM ANOTHER YOU

The Mayans would greet each other by saying "In Lak'ech," which translates to "I am another you." They understood the value of humility amongst their people as they chose to speak its virtue into existence each time they engaged and interacted with one another. Our thoughts become our conversations. Our conversations shape the perception of our shared reality. What starts in our thoughts and minds becomes the consequence we experience circling around in our lives. If we learn how to win the wars within ourselves, we can win the wars in our reality. When we transcend suffering, self-actualize, and hold presence, we can think, speak, and act with *humility* as the foundation of our way of being.

> In humility, there is no separation.
>
> In humility, there is no illusion.
>
> In humility, there is no ego.

Humility offers us a virtuous center for a moral life. It helps us understand that we are not higher or better than anyone else, it teaches us that we are all equal and unique. You are not perfect, and you must realize that nobody is, we are all just other people of the same level of divinity walking this earth together. Do not confuse humility with weakness, or meekness, it simply helps us remove ourselves from being the center of the equation to realize that we are part of the sum.

We must make humility a *practice* because it is not something that naturally occurs. Our ego will always attempt to pull us into a story of self-importance that blinds us from having respect and empathy for one another. We practice humility by engaging ourselves in the discipline to actively choose it. You must acknowledge that we can have misperceptions of our unknowns, meaning that you do not know everything, and you are not as smart as you think you are. We practice humility by developing a light curiosity for other people's perspective and revealing vulnerabilities to ourselves and others. This helps foster better connections and relationships because the energy exchange is purely transparent and open.

When practicing humility, you access deeper levels of compassion when engaging with other people. This will help your daily interactions have more *weight* to them. With humility we can go beyond the "small talk" we normally use and communicate from a higher consciousness on personal, emotional, and relational levels. This lights you up throughout your day as all your interactions carry higher vibrations.

We need to infuse our humility into our humanity, and it starts as small as with ourselves. Only those who have humility can give it. Choose to connect to the virtue of humility and be an abundant source as you live out your life. Be a symbol for the power of humility through your connection to self.

INTUITION – OUR CONSCIOUS GUIDE

As everything in this Universe is energy and works in energy exchange, our intuition is our superpower of *sensitivity* we develop that interprets, reads, understands, and interacts with the energy of our environments to help guide our decisions.

In elevating our intuition, we can sense the vibrational energy of ourselves relative to the energy of everything else, and the energy of everything else relative to our energy. Through the power of our intuition, we can transmit and receive energy through low and high frequencies that influence reality. The level of our influence is dependent upon the strength of our present consciousness. There are levels to growing this ability, and we grow our intuition stronger through daily connection and practice.

In a deep connection to our intuition, we realize the power that can be channeled by our knowledge and emotional intelligence.

Developing a balance of our logic and emotion can help you have profound communication with the subtle energies in your environment. Intuition is your higher *knowing*, your higher intelligence that guides your experience of life through the doors that conspire to *awaken* you.

In the dissolving of our ego and the unraveling of madness from our spirit, we begin to quiet and control the voice that clouds our intuition from breaking through and guiding our decisions. We start to feel and hear our gut feelings, our second brain, the enteric nervous system. Comprising of the same neutrons and neurotransmitters found in the central nervous system, our second brain is our gut and has a direct line of communication to our brain. This plays a key role in having the truth of our ideas, inspirations, insights, and connections be more prominent in guiding our internal dialogue to intuitively guide our experience increasingly in the situations throughout our life.

Trusting your gut sharpens the connection to your intuition. The connection each of us have to this inner guidance, inner *knowing* is strengthened by our ability to hear its voice, apply it, because we realize that this is exactly how we live a life truer to the one we dream of. The more we hear it, the more we listen to and for it, the more we use it, apply it, trust it and be guided by it; the more we reveal our truth to ourselves.

This is a critical part of the spiritual awakening process. As you begin to empower yourself by using your intuition you catch the moments your true and authentic self speaks to you within. In hearing this intuitive, loving, abundant and spiritually inclined voice, you can then compare it to the false, limited, hateful, pessimistic, and untrue one. You *catch* yourself when drifting away, you recognize yourself when aligned with truth. Tapping yourself into using your intuition will provide you the connections, a-ha moments, epiphanies, and realizations.

> Through connection and application of your intuition,
> your spirit will intelligently guide you.

THE CATCH — LIVING WITH MIRRORS

"The catch" is the moment you take a step back to realize you are not connected to your truth or self by what you are saying, thinking, or doing in the present moment. You have caught your true self drifting away from who and what you really are. While we are in these states of programmed unconsciousness, we can be deceived to experience forms of suffering. We know that if *we* do not change, *it* will not change, and by *catching yourself,* you take the first step toward making the real changes that end your suffering. This requires a lot of strength to not take it personally when you do realize, and it is best to just forgive yourself and learn how to be better ahead of it from happening again.

> Work to not allow anything to stick, smudge,
> or smear your internal-external reflection.

Once you have broken through the illusions of your experience, it becomes a challenge to remain true and unwavering as you carry this high vibrational frequency from moment to moment without losing yourself in transition. It helps to be aware of your awareness by imaging yourself living with mirrors, as it keeps you locked in the present reality of your mind, body, and spirit while you experience your life.

When we walk with mirrors, we are conscious of our body language relative to the physical environment. We are aware of what we think and speak. We are doing things to be aware of our awareness, so that we will have more of our power to choose and remain true to ourselves. It can also help to visualize a film crew following you around and documenting the extraordinary and inspirational daily actions you take. Know that how you live your day is how you craft your life. In practice of this, we can use our presence to see when we interact with our environment and develop *smudges* and *smears* to our mirrors which disrupt the clarity of our reflections.

You are a masterpiece and a work in progress at the same time.

SPIRALING OUT

Piggybacking off your growing ability to catch yourself when wavering and slipping away, your hold over present moment awareness begins to blossom and show you profound experiences, *epiphanies,* and *realizations.* These deeply meaningful connections of high-level perceptual understandings unite and pave the process of spiraling out. The spiritual journey guides you to a higher level of thinking, a deeper perspective of observing. In this you begin to engage and perceive reality in new ways, observing your experience using higher levels of consciousness that show you the universal signs that guide you to your *awakening.* Your journey within is an unravelling, a spiraling out of the false identity, story, and perception of your third dimensional shell.

There are certainly times of struggle while implementing and adapting to the newfound knowledge and changes you make. When we do not upload information to our long-term memory, when we do not keep awareness in our awareness, we tend to relapse back into comforts of the old ways that cause our suffering. It is frustrating, but only until you realize each struggle and challenge is a wise teacher in disguise. We hold fast by having *integrity and complete ownership.* For instance, you may have to learn the lesson of discipline a few times before it is truly accepted into your perception. Sometimes it requires many different situations to teach us the same lesson before we realize it's sacred message. Maybe the fourth or fifth time you go through a cycle of suffering where discipline is once again the wise teacher and answer, you realize that you may have just needed to learn it on a deeper level, than the not so challenging times discipline showed you its wisdom. Sometimes struggling with an already learned lesson brings us to a deeper meaning with it that truly evolves our knowledge and understanding in a way that our highest self needed. As your self connection grows deeper on this spiritual journey, so does your perspective and this means that when you get yourself to a whole other level than before, sometimes you must reflect on the learned lessons that got you there to see how they can be applied on this next level depth of perception. The lessons that teach you along the journey apply to each level you continue to ascend to.

A lack of integrity is the gap between what you say and what you do. It is an especially important part of the spiraling out process to learn to live in integrity with yourself. If what you say and what you do are two different things, then you are inevitably going to fall back into cycles of suffering. Integrity is an asset to you on the spiritual journey because it gives you the power to carry you through the darkest depths of hell and back. When we live in integrity, we do not have to even consider the idea of regretting our decisions and actions. You know you are in the moment applying your knowledge and awareness to see doors of opportunity to practice your higher-level consciousness. You want to see the bad within you and throughout you so that you can see and absolve the madness through your growing powerful connection to self.

Own up to everything. You must have complete ownership for everything in your world as you spiral out. If there's relationships you are not nurturing, self-love you are not practicing, look at all the dimensions of your life and be as honest with yourself as possible when you self-reflect upon the changes you make. Learn to master the art of *rebalancing* your focus and energy to compensate for the shifting dynamics that change brings. If you neglect to have ownership of your thoughts and actions, there will be no harmony. Really look at the big picture to see where your energy and focus can be borrowed and given for rebalance.

EPIPHANIES AND REALIZATIONS — THE FIRST CLICK

Our epiphanies and realizations on the spiritual journey are sudden manifestations of deeper levels of perception. Not to be confused with totality of enlightenment, but a budding intuitive grasp on reality through seeing the signs of the Universe as we are guided by *synchronicities* that *illuminate* your thoughts to have profound and personal discoveries and realizations. Your knowledge and life experiences connect and merge together to give you a deeper understanding and perspective.

These illuminations come from the unique connections we make between our old program's knowledge and understanding base to our blossoming higher levels of consciousness. As we reflect and explore more about ourselves and what we do not know, we become privy to access higher levels of thinking and seeing. The deeper and wider we see and think, the more we reveal ourselves to our truth.

You might be lying in bed, standing at a bus stop, or seated in a meditation when suddenly…

Click.

It hits you. Your higher levels of consciousness create a connection that only you can understand. A link between something personal and deeply profound that shifts the entire dynamic of your understanding of yourself, life, reality, and the Universe. They are the keys that unlock a cheat code within our DNA that gives us wisdom to navigate our experience of life in spiritually enriching ways. A jewel of knowledge that teaches you a wise lesson.

I remember the very first epiphany I ever had shocked my entire state of being into the highest vibrations I had ever felt. It happened when I had a few thoughts connect and guide me to a deeply realized dimension of wisdom, I felt like my whole body was buzzing with electricity. I was elated and illuminated that I had discovered this profound knowledge within my own thinking by fusing a few pieces of information to create a deeply profound understanding. It felt like I had hacked into a mind cheat code that gave me access to the ability to expand my level of thinking. I could see from a higher view because I had made a realization that put me ahead of the old me that would fall under illusions put out into the world.

After that first epiphany, I questioned a lot more because I had never experienced nor felt anything like this before. I knew deep down that I was starting to catch on to something, but it was not clear to me at the time what that was. Then I had another epiphany, then another. I began pulling away layers of useless psychology that were being replaced by higher and higher levels of thinking.

We are gifted with these epiphanies and realizations to resolve the remaining layers of our misunderstandings and discontents so we can transcend beyond our cycles of suffering. With epiphanies, we guide ourselves to end the unnecessary suffering we experience. Once something hits us so deep and you *know*, there is no need to continue in cycles of suffering, so why would you?

> We are guided to enlightenment through our realizations and epiphanies.

The timing of my daughter's birth was integral to one of my most profound epiphanies along my spiritual journey. The day we had brought her home for the first time, I had a moment when I looked at her and saw the indescribable purity and innocence of what we all are as we are born into this world as. I could see the quintessential blank slate and infinitely possible blissful life that we are gifted with, and I could not help comparing this to all the suffering and chaos we see and become.

I could see the contrast and choice of the world of happiness and joy, and the world of hurt, of heartbreak, of pain and suffering. As I had this moment with my daughter, I reflected on my own desire to have this peace and in that moment, I realized; I have the power to control and reset my mind, I had the power to gift myself a rebirth to this purity. What was standing in the way of this? It was only an illusion, a false belief that denied me from feeling as content as her. So many of my "problems" seemed so irrelevant in comparison to putting my energy in the direction of feeling like this. I decided to stop fighting against the simple truth of *letting go*.

This epiphany had me forever realize that it was only my narrow perspective that was denying me the acceptance of my own purity and high vibrance. Throughout my unaware and unobserved life up until that point, I had conditioned and limited myself away from a series of false beliefs and illusions that were not serving me. My daughter showed me in that moment the wisdom that I must not allow any situation or circumstance to make me become who and what I am not.

I saw the impact and influence that comes from our environment and that I had a choice in doing something about it. I could see that if I chose to show her and myself a low vibrational and ugly way of being a human, that she might be blinded under the same illusion too. I began to understand the incredible power of our thoughts and actions and how they direct the energy that attracts and manifests the world around our focus. I realized that we can be taught and conditioned to be depressed, anxious, or angry, just as we can be taught how to be happy and intentional. The gift of this epiphany was understanding the power of choice. Tapping into this personally powerful discovery, I chose to ground myself to holding onto this epiphany, to recall it and remember the lesson it was teaching me so that I would not lose its insight as I would continue journeying deeper into my self-connection with spirituality. You will experience epiphanies just like this that will forever change you, and it is important to have a way to bring yourself back to remembering the depth of their teachings.

> **Keep your eyes open to the world teaching you what will heal you.**
>
> **You are one realization away from a completely different life.**

THE GOLDEN RATIO — CLICK, CLICK...BOOM!

Our epiphanies and realizations begin blossoming and fusing together, growing, and expanding our understanding of truth and unraveling us closer to ourselves. All energies that you put into this journey, all knowledge you have accumulated begins to alchemize, compound, and intertwine. An algorithm of higher consciousness begins to form, connecting and correlating your realizations and epiphanies to deeper truths and illuminations.

The golden ratio comes from the mathematical *Fibonacci sequence*. This sacred geometry merges the laws of mathematics and the essential structure of nature. This sequence starts with 0, then 1, and the subsequent numbers are the sum of the previous two.

0, 1, 1, 2, 3, 5, 8, 13, 21, 34, 55, 89, 144, to *infinity*.

Our spiraling out process works under the same principles of this mathematical sequence.

As the spiritual journey connects you to realizations and epiphanies of psychology, biology, quantum physics, physiology, to nature, the Universe, and *everything*; this subsequently spirals you beyond forms of suffering and madness. These connecting epiphanies open you to further access higher dimensions of consciousness. You ascend the levels of consciousness until...

Click, Click...Boom!

You experience a *satori*. An awakening of monumental proportions. A divine intervention. A sudden inner intuitive experience of *enlightenment*. It is unexplainable, indescribable, and unintelligible. This experience pushes you to the edge, to take a leap of faith, a moment of complete self-surrender.

The moment of self-surrender is to die before you die.

The moment of surrender pushes you to symbolically *die before you die*. The experience of an ego death has you personally realize for yourself that death is the ultimate illusion keeping us from understanding that we are *infinite* and *eternal beings*. By facing your mortality, you can realize that we are something beyond our human identity, our higher consciousness is something much *greater*.

Ego death gives us perspective and perception beyond the illusions of identity. Beyond ego we can see connection rather than separation. An ego death is highly personal, highly emotional experience that forever sheds the skin of who you are not by shifting your awareness to deeply know thyself.

The ego death I experienced allowed me to stand at the edge of everything that had tortured and troubled my spirit and experience of life. Ego death gifted me the sight and understanding of knowing what the most fundamental source of our existence is. By questioning my own existence, I was pushed to an edge where I was willing to take my own life, willing to lose it all, and because of this, it gave me an experience where I could see beyond the painful lens of ego.

My spouse and I had just dropped off our son for a weekend with the grandparents. This was supposed to be our reconnecting, romantic weekend filled with peace and serenity. The idea was to enjoy each other outside the roles of parenthood for the first time in a while. On the drive back from dropping our son off, something struck a nerve, and we got into a serious and intense argument. I remember for the last ten minutes of the drive we stopped speaking to each other entirely. Once we got home, we went our separate ways in our house and pretended as if we did not exist to each other. For the rest of the night this continued and even into the next morning when she left for work without speaking to me. There was a dark tension between the two of us unlike anything we had experienced before. I had the day to myself, but I remember feeling so guilty, numb, deflated, and vibrationally low.

To this day I do not understand where this thought came from, but I had begun to contemplate the idea of putting rat poison in my drink. My thought process was I could end my life and "that'll show her!" A few hours later, I went to the kitchen to fill my cup with some water and the idea of stirring in the rat poison came into my focus once again. I looked over at the cupboard underneath my sink and realized it was right within my reaching distance to do it. I realized that I could make this happen right now and no one would be able to stop me. A part of me really wanted to die at that moment. I then visualized myself reaching down, opening the cupboard, grabbing the rat poison, and stirring it into my drink. I snapped outside of this visual and took a sip from my cup. Something came over me and my hand began to tremble, and I could see the water rippling inside my cup. For a moment

I questioned what was real. I began to *believe* that I had poisoned myself and that my life was about to end.

I fell to the kitchen floor and curled into the fetal position, and this is when everything went black. I began to see my entire life flash by on an incredible non-linear timeline. I saw the good, the bad, the ugly and all the connections to all the people I had loved and met throughout my life. I then saw the web of people I had close relationships with receive the news that I had taken my own life. This was in my focus because at the time I was receiving news every month that another close friend had made the choice to take their own life. This visual made me feel something I never had felt before that I was loved by a large amount of people. I remember coming to my senses again, and as I got off the floor, I went directly outside to sit in the corner of my back porch and stared out over the entirety of my beautiful backyard. I sat there for a few hours in an existential trance thinking about all the memories of my life. My spouse had then come home from work and walked right by me without even looking, as if I were not even there. I began to question if I even was *there*. As she went through the door and walked into the house, I imagined a sudden and painfully loud scream that made me cover my ears and tuck my head into my lap. I had visualized my spouse entering the house seeing my body lifeless on the kitchen floor covered with blood and vomit all around me. I saw flashes of her breakdown in tears screaming "WHY!," calling 911, and having the paramedics place me in a body bag and carry me out of the house and off to the morgue. I then saw time go by as a future reality that went on without me and how my decision to take my own life had changed and impacted the world I lived in and the people I love. I witnessed decades into the future from the consequence of my actions and saw how selfish an act it was that I committed.

This visual felt so real until I realized it was not. I had snapped back to the present moment reality like I had never been in it before. For the first time in my life, I felt *hyper*-aware in a state of super consciousness. I remember the moment feeling so remarkable that I was alive, one with everything and that empowered me to change anything, be anything, and to create anything. I realized the gift of life in a way I had never felt before. Like the movie "It's a wonderful life" (Capra, 1946) I approached my spouse with such joy and exhilaration that I was still alive, I was still with her, and I apologized for everything that happened between us. I had broken through the other side to see the blissful celebration of life. When I came to and explained to my spouse everything that I had just seen and been through, we had a moment of embrace that strengthened our connection to a depth like never before, she could feel the shift that happened within me.

This experience of ego death I had gone through expanded my perception beyond the story that was limiting my experience of life. I was so grateful that my life was not over, and everything then seemed like *extra,* as if I escaped death and this life that I experience, live, and create in was on bonus time. I felt like I had nothing to lose by living out my life in deep connection with my truth. That life was a true playground for my spirit to operate and express itself fully and joyfully. Gaining this awareness forever changed my life, because I had access to a higher consciousness that resonated on the higher frequencies of empathy, gratitude, unconditional love, and oneness of all things.

As each drop of water in the ocean is not separate from the rest of the ocean, our consciousness is not separate from divine consciousness. We are all from the same source.

You realize the life you have been living, the program you have been running on, the problems you have, the toxic habits and patterns you recognize relative to the *satori* you experience, pushes you to a point where there is a moment of **faith** to *fully surrender.* You jump off the cliff and build your parachute on the way down. You believe in yourself and live like you are already dead.

From this moment, you transcend as the eternal being having a human experience. To live illuminated and enlightened with source energy and intelligence flowing through you.

> What may seem like the end,
> is a new beginning.
>
> A transcendence, a metamorphosis, a rebirth.
>
> The death of our suffering is the birth
> of our connection to divine oneness.
>
> Universal unconditional love.
>
> Once we awaken, we shift our consciousness
> into the fifth dimension of being.

PROTECTING YOUR ENERGY

The end of suffering gives new life and energy to your mind, body, and spirit. It is wise to reflect on the ways that protect this energy, so you do not become inundated and intoxicated by unwanted vibrational frequencies from entering your domain. It helps to envision a protective bubble around your energetic aura. So, wherever you go, whatever you do, nothing interrupts nor gets in the way of your energetic connection to high vibrational frequencies.

You protect your energy when you:
- Enjoy your own company.
- Use the power of aloneness to meditate and align to your authenticity.
- Do not entertain vibrations not serving you.
- Pay attention to what brings you down.
- Make yourself a magnet for high vibrational energy.

- Stick to the routine that fills your cup.
- Speak up when others are crossing your energetic boundaries.
- Eat food with high vibrational energy.
- Let go of distractions not serving you.
- Do not accept a complacent, aimless, and mediocre life.
- Go into nature and connect to what is real.
- Are honest with yourself.
- Learn the power of saying "no" to people and events.
- Are real and honor your emotions by expressing them openly.

Remember that this energy you have is *powerful beyond measure* and serves as a protector for you. When you own this power, other people's toxic and negative vibrations are not going to easily override and penetrate through your deep connection to self and truth. The most fundamental way to protect your energy is to replenish, align, and balance it.

> **We must protect our energy out of love and not fear.**

THE POWER OF TIME

Time is an illusion constructed by our human minds. We speak, think, and use time on a linear scale to coordinate and collaborate in our daily lives out of convenience. Time dissects our experience of life into minutes, hours, days, and years becoming the interpretations and expectations of what and when we should be doing things. We use *this* time for sleep, and *that* time is meant for work, and in doing this, we begin to place a container over ourselves and become trapped by the illusion of clocks and numbers.

We can understand how to use the laws of time once we elevate our consciousness to the fifth dimension of being. Seeing time as a tool. We maximize and master time when we use our energy and focus to create in the reality of now. Coupling with the power of quantum mechanics, we learn to bend and alter time in our favor.

It may take you many decades or 10,000 hours of apprenticeship to become a master. After years and years of getting it wrong, you figure out how to get it right. Where something that would take months of progress years ago, can now be done in days. This is the power of harnessing quantum mechanics. This empowers you to compound knowledge and make leaps of monumental progress. In using this intelligence, you alter time and bend it in your favor by learning how to rapidly accelerate it.

It is important to value this lesson because as you progress toward mastery, the less you do, the more you get out of it, and this creates you more opportunity for other ventures. It also compounds your overall intelligence, because once you learn from one task or craft, you can then begin applying the same intelligence to other dynamics of your life.

There is no separation between past, present, and future—they happen simultaneously.

The past is now.

The present is now.

The future is now.

So much of our language and phrases are in future tense like when we say, "I'm going to" or "I'll be there" and in doing this we lose our connection to the present moment as we refer to later dates and times. We master time when we change our language to speak in the now. As a practical daily reminder, I took the battery out of the watch I wear. I set the arms of the clock to 11:11 so that each time I look down at my watch, I am reminded of the illusion of time and that the only time is *now*.

COLLECTIVE CONSCIOUSNESS – QUANTUM ENTANGLEMENT & SOURCE INTELLIGENCE

Everything is energy. Energy is light. Light is Consciousness. When transcending our consciousness to the fifth dimension, we can access higher knowledge and intelligence from other realms and higher dimensions. Through *quantum entanglement,* we raise the frequency of the light of our consciousness in meditative states to the frequency level of light consciousness existing in higher dimensions and realms. The atoms of light from your consciousness and the atoms of light from higher dimensions *entangle* once they meet at the same vibrational frequency and on the quantum level, **they begin to communicate**.

In this communication, we connect to *Source Intelligence.* The Universal unified field of consciousness that holds all events, words, emotions, and thoughts that occur past, present, and future, for all time. Transcending consciousness to this level is the *ultimate* connection. It gives your consciousness access to the highest degree of knowledge and intelligence our human brains can comprehend, conceptualize, and articulate. You can openly explore the Universe, by communicating with energy on the other side of the world, from various times and in different dimensions.

In this window, we receive downloads of knowledge, information, intelligence, and empowering states of being from raising our consciousness to access these entanglements.

With this connection we gain the ability
to change the reality around us.

There is a *great awakening* on the rise within our humanity. As more people transcend suffering and separation by elevating their personal levels of consciousness our collective consciousness is waking up to higher levels. Metaphorically, this great awakening happens like microwaving a bag of popcorn. Each kernel pops at various times and when it is ready, just like in each of us awakening to our self and power when the Universe conspires it. Understand that you are not alone in this. There are millions of people around the world right now that are *here* just like you that are raising their levels of consciousness and connecting to the deeper understandings of our Universe and existence.

> **We fall when divided and separated by illusions and constructs.**
>
> **We rise together, connected, united as One.**

FINDING PURPOSE

Once you have reached a point where you have cleansed, healed, and now alchemized the past to transcend you presently and see the future forward, you are left with the decision of what to do with your valuable time and high vibrational energy.

Ask yourself: *Do I know what I want? What do I like to do? What are my dreams? What do I believe I am here on this earth to do?*

If you do not have an answer, look within yourself until you do so that you can live through the meaning and purpose that motivates your thoughts and actions to sacrifice, to pay the price to make the dreams that you have in your mind to bridge and become the reality you experience. Recalibrating your connection to your *why* and *what matters* will help you embrace the inevitable struggles of the dark days and fears that try and stop you from ascending to the next level.

When my spouse became pregnant with our child, it was the connecter that merged us together as family. This was a true blessing in our life, and from that sense of love, I had the deep desire to use what teachings I had learned from my early spiritual journey to bring this brand-new baby into the world in a loving and very nurturing environment. As the Coronavirus was changing the world, I had to be responsible to raise this human to see through the illusions of this world. I wanted to have a massive impact on her life, and give her so much love, and the only way to do that was to be around her as much as possible. I had the option with my career in the army to take parental leave and decided to plan and set this time with her up before she was even born. I had struggled with taking time away from the army because I saw myself as having such an integral role, a key contributor to the overall operation of our missions and duties. I thought that I was too valuable to the guys, that I could not leave them hanging. My heart was torn.

I decided that I only had this one chance to be present for the most impressionable months of my daughter's development, so I chose to step away from my profession and focus on something much more important to me. In having the time with a fresh human being and seeing the world through her eyes with my newly learned patience and unconditional love, and to see the bleach white blank canvas that we start out as, and to then look out at the world and see all the suffering we endure as humans living this life, it caused a shift in my own way of thinking. This time spent on parental leave having this pure and innocent spirit teach me things of who and what we are beyond all the chaos and drama, I had a sudden epiphany that made me realize my purpose on this earth. I knew that my spiritual journey to heal all the wounds I had healed and to be shown the beautiful and blissful side of life had prepared me for my role on this earth. It is to show those who have endured suffering the way forward on the journey, to show them that they can shift their perspective from suffering to bliss. I was chosen to be the alchemist.

After my six-month parental leave was up, I was reluctant to go back to work. I had lived in an environment of love, compassion, empathy, and purity, and now I was stepping back into the world of chaos and violence. As I went back, I noticed that everything seemed just the same as the way it was when I had left it. The army was a green machine that had carried on with or without me. It hit me that I was *replaceable*. I then realized that this replaceability liberated me. It was not what I was passionate about. This was not what gave me energy when I woke up in the morning. It used to be that. It was once everything to me; it just was not anymore. I grew sad because I knew this was the end of something that had been important to me. This was what gave me a foundation, a backbone and I was forever grateful for the life the army had given me, but I just did not feel the same way about it. This chapter for me is over.

I chose to gently make my exit and pursue a life where I would help heal people who suffer and are looking for a way out. Every time I would talk to someone about the move, I was making to go all in on following my dream, I got so elated and felt pure happiness. This was my calling, and I felt so electric living for it every day. Each day I felt free and would just dedicate all my energy to picking up the flag of my progress and do all that was in my power to inch it forward as much as I could. I'd go to bed satisfied that I had done the work necessary to manifest my dream.

With the book's manuscript nearing its completion, I reflected about what I could do with my time to be of higher service to my new mission. I realized that if I wanted to help as many people as possible, I had to get this book in the hands of as many people as possible. To really have the information of this book create the biggest impact, I had to leave my profession to focus on writing. I also had to learn how to make this book a bestseller.

My friends at the time were getting married, and we organized for their parents to meet for the first time in my backyard over a nice autumn fire. When speaking to the husband-to-be's dad, we shared some common ground as he had just left his career with the police force after a twenty-year career as I had just left my career in the army. He told me he recently took an early retirement because of the stress of the job and that the role was not aligned with new personal values, principles, and morals. Again, this was just as the same as why I had left my career. He mentioned he had been selling cars at a dealership for six weeks and was loving the change of scenery. He mentioned his wellbeing had improved in the new workplace environment and this conversation planted a seed in my mind. The next day, I drew up a résumé and knocked on every car dealership's door in town, looking for an opportunity to find the best environment for me to learn the art of sales. I came across a dealership that worked as a team, had online education opportunities, and had great people currently working there. They offered me a spot and I took the job and started my apprenticeship to learn the art of sales and servitude.

This helped grow my confidence with speaking and engaging with people and gave me a greater sense of people and connectivity. I had spent the previous year cooped up in my house not having a great understanding of the outside world I was trying to help. I had successfully infused myself back into the public after going through my *deep* spiritual journey, and as I re-entered the world after this caterpillar, cocoon, butterfly transformation, I was empathetic, patient, loving, kind, and I had found a beautiful way to reintegrate back into society. I took all the lessons I had learned on my journey and found a way to have them benefit others. I knew every day that the better I got at what I was doing, the more people I could help. I had the belief and the manifestation followed.

You must believe that it is possible for you to accomplish your dreams. Believe that it is possible, that you can do it, that you are the greatest, so that you can have permission to be the greatest. It is when our thoughts are backed up with actions that match our beliefs that we can make miracles happen. We dance through this life and make moves like we are unstoppable and on fire. This zone is where greatness is practiced and you achieve higher and higher levels of your skills, abilities, with your talents and gifts.

I became relentless with my work ethic to make this happen, because I knew a lot was on the line. I had been a miserable fuck and blossomed into a blissful life, and I believed there was someone out there that could use my help. I was the only one who could author this book, so I had to write it. I had to help those suffering and seeking answers or else I would forever regret not making this decision. It became my new duty, my new mission that I was the leader and the follower of. The teacher but also forever the student. I poured all the time and energy into it that I could. You do this when it is something that gives you purpose and meaning. You bend the universe to make your dreams a reality.

The mountain you choose to climb will teach you things. It is not easy climbing to the peak of a mountain. Your dreams and desires do not just fall into your lap, they require relentless work, and you must dedicate yourself to what is required to put your vision into practice. You start at the bottom and endure the struggle and this test of strength will get you to the top to only realize what the climb did for you. It brought you to a higher level and the choice is do you settle at this level, or do you keep going because it is not over. There is where you were, and where you are now. So, as you take a moment to celebrate your progress, you will then wonder, what next? Then you realize that this peak you just ascended to is just the bottom of a new summit up the same mountain. You zoom out to see the bigger picture. So, you recognize the growth from the last climb and shift your focus to finding the next height. You climb the beta. The information of the route where the best key holds are, and the sequence one must use for the next successful ascend. Life is this forever enduring sprint and marathon in which you dictate the attitude you have as you climb; you also decide the altitude that you climb. All is your choice. The levels you can go are infinite. The heights you can reach are boundless. This mountain you call life is your worthy sacrifice and the choice is yours in what you do with it. It is a short life and a beautiful opportunity to endless create and dream. The choice is yours. What is your purpose? What do you climb for?

By doing what you enjoy and love, have talents and abilities for, you make yourself useful to the world around you. By doing something that benefits yourself, your family, and humanity as a form of contribution, you find purpose. This is what you wake up in the morning for and leaves your fingerprint on the world.

There may be times where you fall into a funk, lose momentum, and fail hard on the ground. In my experience, these can sometimes serve as the best teachers because after you fall you can get up and recalculate your approach. This fall during your ascend wakes you up to question your process and in this reflection, you may learn something that takes you far beyond the level you were previously at before the fall. Our failures serve us when we do not take it personally and learn from what the experience is teaching us. You will fall many times on your climb, be sure to refine your process and grow yourself to the next level where you turn exposed weaknesses into strengths.

The apprenticeship to become a master starts by working in the shadows. By toughing it out through the dark days, the ones where you don't feel like doing it, when nobody is watching, the days where you question yourself, but this purpose gives you a why, it is what matters deeply to you personally, so you have the strength to remain resilient to continue refining your craft, skills, and abilities. You begin to make leaps of progress as you face your fears by being vulnerable enough to make mistakes and learn from them to continue to grow and evolve. What stops most people and submits them into quitting is fear. Fear is the inhibitor for us to reach the next level of our goals. When we do not back up our pursuit of greatness with accountability and courage because fear is stopping our progress, we open ourselves up to living a life we regret because we do not live it true to our dreams and desires.

You can choose to be content, complacent, and *comfortable* with the current level you are at and have achieved thus far, not putting much energy into expanding and levelling up. You can choose to be *hungry* and do a little more than most. Or you can choose to be **starving** about your purpose and do whatever it takes to show up, do the work, never quit, and use your curiosity to ask the right questions that take you to higher levels. The energy you put behind your purpose is your choice.

Ask yourself: *Where is that fight within me? That burning desire to put your energy toward remarkable things.*

Think of life like entering a boxing match. The bell rings and the other person in the match (life) is coming toward you. What do you do? If you say "I don't know" you wind up stuck in the corner getting pummeled. The question again; where is that fight within you? After a while something deep inside will want to throw a punch. To engage with life in a worthwhile fight where you pursue success and victory with the totality of your infinite and eternal spiritual energy. So, you **find** that fight within you, that *all you got* that is in there, and apply it to an endeavor that is meaningful to you. If you fight like your backs against the wall and bring *all you got* out, if you take this approach to your own life, you will nurture the very spirit *within you*. You begin stalking your day like an animal stalks its prey.

> Your fighting spirit that is starving for success in
> reaching your goals, in pursuing your dreams,
> in living as your authentic self, in being a force
> to promote love, are all different dimensions of a
> higher consciousness, divine intelligence.
> While in pursuit
> of a clear destination, we find meaning and purpose
> for what each of us fight for.

It is important to understand the workings of the Universe in front of you. The paradigm of our reality is in a constant state of change and evolution. It shifts with every event created. Events as big as world wars and with events as small as a thought in your head. As these events are constantly happening, they alter the entire direction of reality. You can be empowered in your higher consciousness when understanding that you are a co-creator of this reality, capable of shifting the direction of it with your energy. It's wise to spend your time and energy shifting your world and reality toward your connection to higher vibrations. By making daily practice of doing what lights you up and engaging and interacting with yourself and people in this vibration, you cause an energetic chain reaction throughout the Universe. We hold the power of creation each as divine messengers of self-connection. Though being who we are, we shift the paradigm of the world and reality into the dimensions of higher consciousness.

Most believe that their existence and actions in this life are irrelevant, as if they are a powerless spec of nothingness. The truth is that you are powerful beyond measure, just like any other being that walks this planet. Transcending consciousness to the fifth dimension of being has you realize we exist as one. Each of us being a unique piece of a monumental puzzle, each a musician playing in the orchestra of the Universe. What we want and are looking for is something that is never set in stone. Our purpose is an active entity that evolves with the passing of time. We are in a perpetual evolution of revealing ourselves to ourselves. The doors and windows you choose as you carve your path will lead you through a subsequent series of events. On and on forever, eternal.

> **Learn to execute at elevated levels**
> **of what you practice every day.**

EVERYTHING IS A VIBRATION

Everything we see, sense and experience has an origin of being an energetic vibrational frequency. It is a fact that all things in this Universe are in motion, constantly *vibrating*. Depending on the speed at which these vibrations travel, it forces the atoms to structuralize and form as matter, the *appearance* of solid, liquid, or gas.

When looking at the science of **cymatics**, we uncover one of the secrets of the Universe, that everything is a vibration. Using a flat steel plate connected to the sound resonance of specific vibrational frequencies and sprinkling a granular substance such as salt on the plate, a remarkable thing happens. As the vibrations move the salt on the plate, it begins to form into incredible two-dimensional patterns. It changes the shapes and patterns when the frequency played changes, shifting the complete design of the shapes. When specific frequencies are layered on top of each other, usually requiring at least five different frequencies, the most astonishing thing happens, a three-dimensional shape begins to form. This means that everything in the perceived universe is held together by a specific combination of energetic vibrational frequencies.

If we know then that everything is operating at some energetic vibrational frequency, including ourselves, we can tap into the power of balancing and raising our own vibration in present moment reality. We can become the thermostat that can set and adjust the climate within ourselves, rather than being the thermometer that only reacts to the cues of our environment. If we learn to tap into the power of elevating the energy with our own selves at a high vibrational frequency, through practicing advanced forms of meditation, we will phase ourselves closer to transcending our consciousness into the fifth dimension of being.

ADVANCED FORMS OF MEDITATION — THE UNIFIED FIELD

You do not understand the incredible experience of transcendental forms of meditation until you experience it for yourself.
- David Lynch

Science and technology now show us the deepest elements of matter in our Universe. Wood, metal, water, and every other physical form existing in our universe are made up of a structure of molecules. Within molecules there are atoms, within atoms there are electrons, neutrons, and protons. Through quantum physics we can venture below the subatomic particles, to the very origin of creation, the unified field. All particles and forces of energy are born from this unified field. From no-thing, from un-manifest, to everything that manifests. The origin of creation for all things in our Universe begins in the unified field.

The deeper levels of matter correspond to the deeper levels of consciousness. As we grow our levels of consciousness, we begin to bring ourselves to the infinite consciousness, the unbounded, immortal, and eternal. We access our higher creativity, intelligence, love, energy, power, and experience our own forms of bliss. Consequently, our negativity retracts, we experience less stress, less anxiety, less depression, less fear, and anger. As we experience deeper forms of meditation, we find the keys that open doors to expand our consciousness.

Through transcendental meditation, an out of body experience, astral projection, or accessing the akashic records, source intelligence, collective consciousness, we dive into the origin of our consciousness and all matter, the unified field. Deeper than concentration and contemplation, we realize the *atman*, the self, the essence of life itself. We know ourselves by being it, through a process of unraveling the layers of who we are not to live as our infinite potential.

We journey our consciousness to higher dimensions and realms and these transcendental experiences show us important teachings for us on our spiritual journey. Much of what we see, sense and experience are the symbols and metaphors for us to perceive, cleanse, and purify some dimension of consciousness from blocking our being's high energetic frequency. We are repeatedly shown lessons such as humility, patience, empathy, and gratitude until they are permanently accepted and present in our energetic vibrational state of being.

Through advanced forms of meditation, we guide ourselves to experience the Tao, Chi, God, the kingdom of heaven, self, truth, enlightenment, nirvana, bliss, however you choose to perceive it. As we transcend our consciousness to the depth of the unified field of the Universe, we become the light that illuminates the world and reality. We end any form of suffering in our experience when we grow and connect our consciousness to this unified field because it provides us with the answers, we set out to seek in this spiritual journey.

Once you know, you know.

All your answers are found within you.

INFINITE BLISS, LOVE, AND ONENESS

This spiritual journey brings us to finding the process to practice our lives, ending the suffering within our mental, physical, and spiritual experience of human life. We elevate our experience of consciousness to the fifth dimension of being by connecting with and guiding our choices and decisions through our intuition, transcending our fears and doubts to have the courage and resiliency of our warrior spirit, and empower our perception by practicing seeing through the lenses of loving empathy and gratitude. We open our eyes, see deeper and begin to see the signs coming from the Universe. The synchronicities, the realizations, the epiphanies that begin to fuse together, and broaden our perception for everything as we walk through the doors of opportunity and remove the limitations from ourselves, from the enslavement to our identity and story we once clung to. We transition our experience beyond suffering, beyond the labels, constructs, lies, and illusions of the third dimensional reality. We can reconnect to our higher consciousness until the moment everything **clicks,** and life fundamentally changes after. It is wise to make daily practice of what you learned on your spiritual journey. Through every thought and action, we create our lives and world.

The higher dimensions connect our consciousness to be in blissful love and see collectively as one. Through raising our meditation practice to transcendental levels, we develop our ability to access source intelligence in higher frequencies. Downloading messages into our DNA, providing us with truth, wisdom, and *knowledge.* You see and connect to the element of the divine within us in a unique way that brings you closer to knowing who and what you really are. You live in your power, continuing to evolve and grow, as there is no end. There is nothing to chase being present in the fifth dimension. You make your life a daily practice of remaining highly conscious of being your true self living in the present moment. When this practice is executed by you at an elevated level, and you make it *normal* to be in this extraordinarily powerful state of being, you enter the 5th dimension. By making it effortless to remain connected to the infinite potential of the present moment that exists, you phase into the fifth dimension without any sort of warning or cue.

In this state, your entire experience of life shifts again in a monumental way. The transcendence of our consciousness to the fifth dimension of being is the death and end of our suffering. Under no veil of illusion, separation, or lies, we live under the perception, paradigm, and prism of higher consciousness, we experience unconditional love, blissfulness, and oneness as our real, true, authentic self.

> The wisdom, knowledge, and information spoken about in this book is not exclusively for the mystics, sages, or wealthy top percenters. We are all equal opportunity to this knowing. Each of us is part of the blueprint of the cosmos. Most people on this earth are sold on a lie of illusion but the truth is we all know we are infinite, eternal, and powerful beyond measure.

Since completing the course with Tony Robbins, I have tried to find new ways to use it to help others who might be in the same situation and circumstance as me, who were suffering in their experience but had no idea where to start, had reluctance or embarrassment for seeking self-help. I wanted to make self-help approachable. I went to the local newspaper on our army base and began writing a weekly article about self-empowering information. This really helped me dive deeper into my own problems and issues and used the wisdom that was most recently serving to me to be put out there for anyone who could benefit from it. Doing this month after month, even while being deployed overseas gave me a deep sense of purpose.

At the time I was just doing and following whatever felt like the best thing I could be doing to grow myself and help those around me. From the newspaper article, I switched my focus to creating my own t-shirt brand. I used the powerful messages that were guiding me through my transformation and put them on a shirt coupled with a metaphorical image that was just as bold. I had previously had experience making T-shirts when I was in a band before joining the army, because I was the one responsible and did all the work designing our shirts, having them printed, and set up our merch booth to make gas money to play shows. I did what I had to do to keep the dream of playing music alive. Then I took this same approach when I started my own brand.

The brand gave me an even greater sense of purpose than the newspaper article writing, because this connected me with amazing uplifting conversations during the process of the sale of a shirt. This connection made me feel like I was doing the right thing. As I continued to follow a path that guided me to new endeavors and to higher and higher purpose. I felt amazing setting up my booth and getting in front of people explaining my brand's message, meaning, and intentions. I met some amazing people over the months that I was getting off the ground. I was printing the shirts in Canada while deployed in Latvia, and when I came home for a mid-tour break, I packed my suitcases full of my shirts and brought them back to sell to people I was meeting on the deployment. There were twelve different countries actively being represented working together on this deployment and I saw a lot of opportunities in that to make connections with people from all over and around the world. This endeavor became my living breathing passion. I was hauling shirts around with my heart and good intentions and backing it up with hustling like crazy, I loved it! I continued to carry the momentum and success I was having from starting this brand, and once the deployment ended and came home, I began seeking better avenues to connect with more people. I entered a wellness expo in a major city and really started to find success with creating this message and brand.

Two weeks after this wellness expo peaking my confidence to really take my brand to beautiful places, the world was suddenly locked down due to the COVID-19 pandemic. My entire business model of getting in front of people, sharing my story, my message was suddenly blocked by not being able to be around other people. I attempted to shift my focus to promoting online but lost my energy because I was pursuing likes and follows more than I was trying to help people. This provided me with the time to take a step back and really question how I could create a *bigger* impact. I started writing some of the most impactful things that were helping me and realized that so many books I had read had helped me, and that I too should author a book to help others while my brand was put on hold.

I shifted my focus over the years of my life from being in a band to joining the army, from writing in a local newspaper to starting a t-shirt company, and now I had the vision to author a book about the spiritual awakening journey and process that just gave me every answer that I was looking for. I knew why I was miserable now. I knew why I was suffering, and it was because I was living a life untrue to myself. I was tormented by the regrets of what I did not do and tortured by what I knew I should do but did not. When I went through the spiritual journey, I found myself and my truth was telling me that authoring this book was the reason I was placed on this earth. Many meditations and guides were there on my dark days, the ones when I thought this was a stupid idea or if I should even do it. There were so many days I wanted to quit. I could never quit because I knew what I was fighting for. I was sick to my stomach hearing people around me committing suicide and living in low vibrational states. I understood that I was sacrificing for something *beyond* myself. Something of great meaning and purpose, I had realized that in writing and publishing this book that I was shifting my deepest desires and dreams to become a manifested reality and it was electrifying.

I felt like an artist painting whenever I could sit down to write. I could collect my thoughts, get them down and put them together in such a way that helped me so much and knew that this information could not only help me but also someone else out there. For anyone, anytime looking for answers but not knowing where to look or where to start, this was the roadmap for anyone feeling lost. I created this book because it is exactly what I would have wished to have been handed to me when I started my spiritual seeking journey. To come full circle, I went from the curiosity of why I was miserable to the creation of living through my true self's purpose. My own path grew and evolved, just following my intention to contribute something using my heart and story that would be of high impact for humanity. I was guided by my purpose all along. It was something in perpetual growth that led me to *here* and *now*.

You may come to the realization that all the epiphanies you have throughout your spiritual journey begin to close the gap between knowing what to do, and actually doing it. With this knowledge and information shared throughout this book, I invite you to step through the limitations and barriers of suffering the unconscious human condition. I dare you to develop a deep curiosity to solve the suffering you experience in your life. Choose to follow your heart down the path of what feels most intuitive to your highest self and know that that is something in constant perpetual motion and evolution. You will find meaning and purpose in your life by learning and applying what it is to be connected to your true unapologetic and authentic self. Go through this journey and process to find your *self*, live through this loving connection, and you will feel the radiant power rebirth; believing, becoming, and being who and what you really are.

> **If you died today, what would you have done differently?**

REFERENCES

Benton-Banai, 1988. https://www.mtroyal.ca/
IndigenousMountRoyal/office-of-Indigenization-and-decoloniza-
tion/sevengrandfatherteachings.htm

Braden, N. https://www.brainyquote.com/quotes/
nathaniel_branden_163773

Capra, F. 1946. Liberty Films

Carpenter, J. 1988. They Live, Avile Films, Larry
Franco Productions

Dass, R. 1990.Paths to God, Bantam; Revised ed. edition.

Deloria, V. https://www.goodreads.com/quotes/160879-religion-
is-for-people-who-re-afraid-of-going-to-hell

Domire, R. 2020. https://duuf.org/services/
spiritual-enlightenment/

Gunaratana Bhante, H. https://www.goodreads.com/
quotes/603699-mindfulness-gives-you-time-time-gives-you-
choices-choices-skillfully#:~:text=Time%20gives%20you%20
choices.,swept%20away%20by%20your%20feeling.

Fresco, K. https://www.challengeachieved.com/quote/balance-is-the-key-to-everything-what-we-5be401724e84cc73bc1541dc

Ford, H. https://www.goodreads.com/quotes/978-whether-you-think-you-can-or-you-think-you-can-t--you-re

Hoffman, A. https://www.goodreads.com/quotes/10473860-it-gave-me-an-inner-joy-an-open-mindedness-a

Kim, J. *I used to be a miserable f*ck: An everyman's guide to a meaningful life*, 2019, Harper Collins Publisher

Krishnamurti, J. 1960. https://www.brainyquote.com/quotes/jiddu_krishnamurti_107856

Laha, Kirk. 2016. https://www.kosmosjournal.org/article/seeing-wetiko-on-capitalism-mind-viruses-and-antidotes-for-a-world-in-transition/

Leary, T. https://www.goodreads.com/author/quotes/47718.Timothy_Leary

Lenz, F. https://www.azquotes.com/quote/1015687

Link, 2018. https://www.healthline.com/nutrition/fasting-benefits

Lynch, D. 2015. https://www.youtube.com/watch?v=Em3XplqnoF4

Matrix Movie, Morpheus https://www.shmoop.com/quotes/you-take-the-blue-pill-you-take-the-red-pill.html

Mercier, P. 2007. *The Chakra Bible.*

Mitchell, J. 2021. https://www.nature.com/articles/s41591-021-01336-3

Morrison, E. *2022.* https://yogapractice.com/yoga/pratyahara/

REFERENCES

New King James Bible, Matthew 7:7. https://www.bible.com/bible/compare/MAT.7.7-8

Nietzsche, F. https://www.goodreads.com/quotes/137-he-who-has-a-why-to-live-for-can-bear

Ramsey, D. https://www.azquotes.com/quote/761557

Robbins, T. 2016. I am not your guru. Netflix Films

Rohn, J. 1996. https://www.goodreads.com/quotes/1798-you-are-the-average-of-the-five-people-you-spend

Runyan, J. 2014. https://impossiblehq.com/impossible-case-study-sir-roger-bannister/

Schwarzenegger, A, Hall, *Arnold: The Education of a Bodybuilder*, 2006, Simon & Schuster; Reprint edition (January 1, 1993)

Sri Chimnoy https://quotefancy.com/quote/1132406/Sri-Chinmoy-Meditation-means-conscious-self-expansion-Meditation-means-one-s-conscious

Singh, M. 2021. *The 12 Laws of the Universe.* Independently published (Oct. 20 2021)

Stokes, V. 2021. https://www.healthline.com/health/pineal-gland-function

Tate, C. 2021. https://carolyntate.co/the-story-of-the-golden-buddha/

Tew, R. https://www.goodreads.com/quotes/7052761-everything-you-go-through-grows-you

Tolle, E. 2005. A New Earth. Penguin Life

Yeo, A. 2016. https://www.urbanbalance.com/
the-story-of-two-wolves/

Ziglar, Z. https://quotefancy.com/quote/943489/Zig-Ziglar-Your-
input-determines-your-outlook-Your-outlook-determines-your-
output-and

ABOUT THE AUTHOR

DAVID LEE SADAI was a member of the Canadian Armed Forces for nine years serving on two oversees deployments while working with thousands of people from many different countries and cultures. He has deeply explored a wide array of wellness practices, first to manage anxiety and depression and subsequently to expand his spiritual awareness. His aim with *Unraveling Madness* is to help others ease their suffering and find meaning and peace in their life.

He lives in Sprucewoods, Manitoba, with his spouse Stefanie and their children Maya, and Jordan, and their Pitbull Mastiff Tyga.